Some Better Days

Poems and Stories Mostly of the Scottish Highlands

Robert O. Scott

Matador
5 Weir Road
Kibworth Beauchamp
Leicester LE8 0LQ, UK
Tel: (+44) 116 279 2299
Fax: (+44) 116 279 2277
Email: books@troubador.co.uk
Web: www.troubador.co.uk/matador

ISBN 978 1848764 644

British Library Cataloguing in Publication Data.
A catalogue record for this book is available from the British Library.

Typeset in 11pt Bembo by Troubador Publishing Ltd, Leicester, UK

Matador is an imprint of Troubador Publishing Ltd

Printed in Great Britain by the MPG Books Group, Bodmin and King's Lynn

'The way was long, the wind was cold,
The Minstrel was infirm and old;
His wither'd cheek and tresses grey
Seem'd to have known a better day.'
From - 'The Lay of the Last Minstrel',
by Sir Walter Scott

This book is dedicated to the memory of my wife, Eileen,
who loved Assynt and its people.

CONTENTS

PART ONE

Some Early Years

Summer Holiday
(Girvan, 1938)

What excitement when, at long last, that horse-drawn
railway cart rumbles to our house door;
how huge that Clydesdale horse,
how bravely its iron-shod hooves strike
lighting flashes of sparks from assaulted cobbles.
As horse, cart, and our hamper are lost to sight
we fear our holiday hamper might be lost
or stolen, might never re-appear in time for our
annual Glasgow Fair holiday 'doon the water'
at Girvan on the wide estuary of the Clyde.

Somehow the dreary waiting days pass
and at last we excitedly hurry from Girvan's
railway station down towards the unseen sea.
Oh how annoying are our parents as, tolerantly smiling, they say,
'You'll see the sea soon. All in good time!'
We turn a corner and there, well remembered from last year,
appears that squat row of hardy fisher-folk's humble homes,
and, yes there is that quaint street name: The Boatie Row;
again it lights a warm anticipatory glow.
We eagerly climb those half worn away,
'half as old as time' steep outside stone steps,
we thunder up bare wooden inside stairs
and from our attic window at last we see the sea.
And there are those same horse-hair chairs
that had so itchily prickled and tickled
the backs of our bare knees and made us boys long
to be old enough to wear long trousers.

Early next morning we hurry to something
almost as exciting as the waiting sea and sand...
The enticing wonders of a large toy shop.
How our few bright, impatient shillings clink and jingle
in our pockets as we near that shop.
What a glorious agony of indecision.. What to buy?
Buckets?... spades?... a large garish beach ball?...
Oh but some new fishing tackle is a must!
But even that is thrust aside by those brave cowboys
resolutely defending their stockaded fort
from fast galloping Red Indians...
see, some have already 'bit the dust'
and how wondrously tempting are those warplanes
that fly high on almost invisible threads
tantalizingly just out of reach above our heads
where pale blue British biplanes fight desperate dog-fights
with the Red Baron's greatly feared 'Knights of the Air'
in their bright red triplanes.
Despite all these tremendous temptations we finally decide
that some new fishing tackle must come first.
That wise decision is quickly vindicated as,
with bare feet dangling and browned legs warming
against sun-mellowed old harbour wall, we keenly watch
many fish dart about in synchronized shoals;
then there's extra excitement that ignites primeval shouts,
that sends inherited instincts soaring
as trembling hands haul up our wriggling haul.

Leaving the harbours mingling, lingering special scents
of spilled paraffin, the tangy tingle of tarry-ropes
and the pleasant, lip licking, salty taste of brine
we enjoy some sedate donkey rides and then some more
adventurous; more jolting trots over firm wet sands.
There's much urgent licking of fast melting ice-cream cones;
large, elaborate sandcastles are lovingly made,
small sailing boats navigate our castle's tidal moats,
bright flags flutter over our castle's highest tower.
Suddenly all play is forgot as excited boys rush to a higher spot
to better see three sleek grey warships steam past;
both boys wave and cheer these warships brave White Ensigns,
both are innocently unaware of their parents fears as,
all too well, they guess what these naval exercises foretell...
The inexorable advance of the grim threat of war.

Our days of simple innocent play continue,
our holidays hours speed by as if in a delirious daze.
We think life can hold no greater pleasures, until we hear
a cry go up: 'Large shoals of mackerel are near!'
We go on a wondrous fishing trip on a real fishing-boat
crewed by real, mahogany tanned, thick-jerseyed fishermen
who steer us to where the sky is alive with dive-bombing gannets.
Such excitement as, staring amazed with mouths agape,
we see suicidal mackerel fling themselves at our
multi-coloured feathered hooks,
then how ancestral fishing hunting nerves vibrate
with trembling wonder as we haul these fish up
in a brilliant glitter of streamlined rainbowed shapes.

Our holiday done, we head for Glasgow on a hurrying,
smoke -belching train;
understanding parents try to cheer dejected children
by promising we will all return to Girvan next year,
and, yes, there will again be large shoals of mackerel.
These unbelieving children are smilingly assured that
one year is not too long to wait,
but these parents, exchanging secret glances, fear
that war might be here before this time next year.

A Historic Day
(3rd September, 1939)

Admonished by our worried father to make no noise
we two boys silently fidgety sit and impatiently wait
for the valves hidden in our new-fangled wireless to
warm up. Soon – perhaps dramatically at high-noon –
we, and all the anxious waiting British Nation
will learn our fate.
The Prime Minister is to broadcast a historic message...
Will he, once more, assure us that his brilliant diplomatic skills
have achieved 'Peace in our Time', or will he give the expected,
the deeply dreaded announcement that we are to go to war?

Solemn music suddenly ends, an oh so correctly accented
B.B.C announcer comes on: 'The Prime Minister will speak
to the Nation now.'
Neville Chamberlain dolefully confirms our worst fears as he
concluded his historic broadcast:
'... and, consequently, this Nation is now at war with Germany!'
Our tearful sister hugs the reassuring warmth and strength
of our always reliable, vastly compassionate mother.
We two brothers wonderingly meet our father's anguished gaze
as, remembering the last World War (that war to end all wars!)
with all its atrocious horrors, he wonders how long this
new war will last....
will it insatiably claim these two boys as cannon fodder?

The youngest brother, much too excited by the novelty of
this state of war, cannot, like the others, sit and wonder
what tragic fate might await them all.
His smiling mother agrees with his desperate pleading;
no matter what precious freedoms this war might take away
surely we must ensure there's always time for childhoods
innocent play.
He is given permission to go out, and even in his desperate hurry
he remembers to take his recent issued gasmask with him.
He meets up with schoolboy friends who excitedly
discuss this war. They naively hope it will not end
before they grow up and become old enough to join-up
and play some part in defeating that evil villain - Hitler.

As they run these boys carefree laugh as their gasmasks,
in their cardboard boxes, dangle on long strings
from thin shoulders and eagerly fly up then cheekily
bump down on each bum.
They follow by the railway track to Cardonald Station
where a special train impatient waits to take evacuees
to the hoped for safety of the Scottish countryside.
The crowded station is a bedlam of chaotic movements
with bemused wide-eyed babes; weeping infants,
loving hugging young mothers; some mothers-to-be;
some auld, stoic, tartan shawled Glasgow Grannies.

As they wave that smoke-belching train away
these cheering boys think themselves very brave
to stay on in Glasgow to face whatever the Hideous Huns
might be going to fling at this tough, warm-hearted old city.
Proud of their keen aircraft-recognition skills
they wonder will they soon see, and correctly identify,
Heinkels and Junkers?
And will these Luftwaffe planes drop not just high explosives,
but also – as many dread – lethal poison gasses?
And might murderous Nazi paratroops also soon descend?
Again they anxiously wonder will this war come to an
unglorious end before they're old enough to play a
meaningful part in helping to defeat Adolf Hitler?

These wondering boys now hear what might be the rumble
of distant thunder; or might those rumbling sounds be the
more menacing thunder of exploding Hun bombs?
Then with alarming suddenness something – perhaps a flash
of lightning – explodes a tethered barrage-balloon
into a flaming, flaring, violent falling dangerous menace.
When a second barrage-balloon violently explodes
and falls in a vivid cascade of vertical fireworks these
boys feel certain that the Jerries must be shooting them down,
but what are they shooting them down with?

There's been no wailing air raid warning,
no revealing sound of enemy planes, so these boys decide
that those Jerries must have some secret weapon.
One boy – an avid reader of H. G. Wells – declares; 'Those
fiendishly clever Huns must have developed a secret,
a deadly dangerous, ray-gun!'
A few warning drops of thundery rain send these boys
hurrying for home before their gasmask's cardboard boxes
become soggily saturated.
As he hurries homeward that imaginative boy
wonders how many more of H. G. Well's fantastic
science-fiction predictions might this war bring about.

'It's One of Ours!'
(Glasgow, Autumn, 1940)

Football playing schoolboys hear the drone of an approaching plane;
as there's been no air-raid warning's familiar wail
there's no fear as the unseen plane's sound growls louder,
then, going into a steep dive, its roaring thunder
rips the shrouding clouds asunder and excited boys
wildly wave, loudly cheer and shrilly shout:
'It's one of ours!... It's a R.A.F. Blenheim bomber!'
Delight turns to dismay as sinister black crosses are seen
on the thundering plane's wings.
All is wild disarray, excited talk stops,
some frightened boys flop, some stand their ground,
one shouts out: 'It's a Heinkel!'
Others violently disagree: 'No, it's a Junkers!'
The plane's machine-guns hammer out a vicious message
then foolishly standing, foolishly staring horrified boys
see two bombs untidily tumble out.

Now every boy's face presses into wet grass
and every trembling body hugs the turf
with the urgency of a lover's lusty embrace
while these Jerry bombs terrify with their eerie
devilish whistle.

The noise of exploding bombs rumbles and echoes then dies;
the plane's drone fades away; numbed, but unhurt, the boys rise.
They greet one another with uncertain nervous smiles,
then, as one, they turn and run to see the two huge
muddily ugly bomb craters that disfigure the far end of this football
field.

Often afterwards, when at school, at home, or out at play
these boys, feeling like their Commando heroes
in the *Hotspur* and the *Rover*, vividly recall–
with many brave additions – that most exciting autumn day.

Glasgow's Last Hansom Cab
(A Story)

'Professor Sutherland's arrived again. He's just gone in to examine that poor frail wee soul, Maggie Campbell.'

My mother's dramatic announcement galvanized me into instant action. I threw back the bedclothes, tumbled out of my sick-bed and, leaping to the bedroom window, breathlessly asked, 'Is his hansom cab waiting for him again?'

Giving a beaming smile that revealed the warmth of her maternal love and her delight at this further proof of how well her thirteen year old son was recovering from his sore throat and feverish cold, my mother nodded and confirmed, 'Aye, son, the professor's cab, horse and driver are all waiting outside our front garden.'

My trembling fingers pulled the dark, thick, war-time blackout curtains wider apart. I eagerly peered through the dense December fog that for most of this chill, windless week had shrouded Glasgow in its sooty mournful pall and there, right enough, was that exciting hansom cab. This cab was not now plying – as it had done in its Victorian heyday – as a horse-drawn taxi, but was the unique private carriage of Professor Sutherland.

This professor was Glasgow's foremost, most renowned expert on this city's worst curse – tuberculosis. This preventable disease was almost epidemic amongst all too many of the impoverished dwellers in Glasgow's worst, most squalid, most overcrowded tenement slums.

His hansom cab had brought the professor from his large Victorian villa in leafy Mosspark to this terraced council house in Drumoyne, a suburb pleasantly distant from the teeming dark grey tenements that crowded around the shipyards of Govan.

As I continued eagerly peering through the obscuring fog with wide, imaginative eyes it seemed impossible that that hansom cab could be a true part of this war-austere city; it seemed completely out of place in this time of wailing air-raid sirens and the deadly threat of the Luftwaffe's devastating bombs. Surely that horse-drawn cab really belonged to, and was fog-linked to Victorian London; it should be waiting, not for Professor Sutherland, but for the world's greatest – and my favourite – detective, Sherlock Holmes!

But then, thinking myself very wise, I surmised that it was not any mere eccentric whim that made the professor use that horse-drawn cab; surely he was conscientiously doing his patriotic duty.

His neat grey horse was only one of many horses brought back into war-time use; his hansom cab only one of many horse-drawn vehicles pressed into service to help save desperately scarce, strictly rationed petrol.

I was correct in what I surmised, but what I did not know was that Professor Sutherland had an extra very strong incentive to patriotically save our hard-pressed Nation's petrol. His brother had been captain of a large oil-tanker and had met a hideous, oil-choked death when his tanker was torpedoed by a German U-boat. And one of the professor's sons was serving in the Royal Navy helping to protect the Atlantic convoys of all types of merchant ships and especially the truly vital, desperately vulnerable oil tankers. Britain's war-effort would grind to a halt if these tankers did not succeed in making their heroic way past the predatory hunting U- Boat Packs.

'Aren't you getting cold standing at that window, son? Don't you want to get back into your warm bed?'

My mother's compassionate voice jolted my imaginative thoughts back from that wondrous hansom cab to the familiar reality of my bedroom. The walls of this small room were bright with my war-time charts and maps. One of these aircraft recognition chart detailed all R.A.F. warplanes; one illustrated every Luftwaffe plane, and – belatedly added – was a chart of all American warplanes. There was a map of Europe and one of the Pacific. Both maps were festooned with small, home-made paper flags. Our old, brought back from retirement, geography teacher encouraged his pupils to make these flags of the Allies and of our vile enemies. These maps and flags served a double purpose. As our pinned flags accurately traced the victorious advance of our Allied heroes and the retreat of our evil foes the progress of the war was made clear to us boys and we effortlessly learned much about the geography of Europe and the Far East.

I reassuringly smiled at my mother, 'No, I'm not cold. No, I don't want to get back into bed. I want to wait and see Professor Sutherland go back into his hansom cab.'

My mother returned my smile and, to my amazement, asked, 'Or is it Sherlock Holmes you're wanting to see get into that cab, son?'

I stared open-mouthed. Knowing almost nothing of the astounding power of a mother's intuitive insights, I could not understand how she could so accurately know what was in my mind.

Giving another warm, understanding smile, my mother said, 'Professor Sutherland or Sherlock Holmes, it shouldn't be long now before one or the other of them come out and trot away.' She did not say so, but she knew it shouldn't take that expert on pulmonary tuberculosis long to examine that poor wee dying lass, Maggie Campbell. That terrible wasting disease had so severe and tenacious a grip on both her lungs that there was little medical science could do to delay that girl's early death.

'I'll go and make you another warm drink, then you'll get back into bed and drink it, all right?'

I nodded and smiled in eager agreement. It *was* getting quite cold standing with bare feet on the cold linoleum in this unheated bedroom.

As I continued peering through the foggy gloom I deeply sympathised with the professor's poor driver as he sat on his high perch at the back of the hansom cab. He must be getting much colder than me. Each time he gave a wheezy, bronchial, fog-irritated cough my recovering, still ticklish throat automatically joined in with a sympathetic wheeze of its own.

Now Professor Sutherland came hurrying out. Tall, slim, elegant, he alertly strode towards his waiting cab. His leather medical case swung from one hand… fittingly it was a rather scruffy, well-used Gladstone bag.

How I wished he had been wearing a tweed deerstalker cap or a glossy top-hat instead of that mundane brown trilby hat. And couldn't he have had a large, curved, meerschaum pipe hanging from his mouth?

The professor threw quick orders at his driver, flung himself into the hansom cab and slammed its door.

The driver gave a word of command, a flick of his whip, and the neat grey horse jolted out of its stoic wait and quickly got into that easy trotting stride that would hurry the professor to the isolated Tuberculosis Wing of the Southern General Hospital. Afterward they would cross the dark, polluted, miasma fogged narrow River Clyde on the large vehicular ferry at Govan Cross and from there go on to Glasgow University's Medical Faculty.

I watched Glasgow's last working hansom cab ghost away into the all enveloping foggy gloom, then as the rhythmic clip-clop of the grey horse's hooves were also smothered by the fog, I leapt back into my cosy bed. I avidly started reading. Soon I was completely engrossed in another Sherlock Holmes story.

No Reply
(Glasgow, 1942)

That telegram boy cycles with easy youthful vigour through
Govan's drab, grey, war-austere streets
and, despite his boss's strict instructions,
went out of his way, eager to see where a Luftwaffe bomb
had landed last night;
perhaps in some deep corner of his mind he wished to delay
delivering the sad message he must relay.

Near the centre of a long tenement row there's
now an ugly gap.
He thinks it's like a grinning mouth
with one front tooth missing.
An unnatural hush pervades this obscene
scene of destruction; some women compassionately sob
while their bairns uncomprehendingly gawk.

That sad old tenement is sliced so deadly neat;
those once cosily private rooms now so indecently exposed;
so many garish contrasting wallpapers;
a pair of wallie dugs – still insipidly simpering – are still
precariously posed on their high, exposed, mantlepiece.

Pushing his bicycle past a high heap of rubble
the telegram boy once again feels the familiar
underfoot crunch of blast-shattered glass.

Blethering housewives fall silent as that telegram boy
turns into their street;
apprehension turns to profound relief as he cycles further on...
Thank God, it's not yet *their* turn to weep!

He stops at number twenty; two middle-age women pale,
they watch with held breath as that small messenger of death
withdraws a telegram from his black leather pouch.
He enquires, 'Mrs. Margaret D. MacPherson?'
Those two women gasp... gasp with relief;
thank God, not their son, their husband!
Relief turns to guilt, to deep sorrow for their neighbour's grief.

'Mrs. MacPherson? Aye, son, first floor, middle door.'
With shy self-importance he starts to climb these old,
worn, tenement stairs; he silently repeats:
'I hope this wifie will not greet.'
It was terrible when they burst into tears...
Have their years of worry culminate in this
realization of their worst fears.

He rings the bell; he undergoes that tense silent wait.
Her face crumples as she sees that small messenger;
she takes that small envelope;
she dreads to guess her fate.
Shaking fingers drop torn envelope; misting eyes read:
' The War Office deeply regrets to inform you–
Killed in action.' Her husband dead!
Duty bound, the telegram boy gently whispers:
'Is there any reply, missis?'
Long, long she stared down with grief-blinded
unseeing eyes; at last she sobs:
'No, son.. No.. No reply!'

Oh for a Sniper's Rifle!
(A story)

Leading Seaman Bill Wainwright was on sentry duty. Confident that their comrade was alertly guarding them, the other four members of this clandestine S.B.S team lay sleeping in the concealment of a small coppice in the Pas-De-Calais region of German – occupied France.

Last night this Special Boat Section team of the Royal Navy had once again successfully completed a dangerous mission. After killing German sentries they had blown up six flying-bombs which were being prepared for launch against London. They then destroyed the launching ramp for these missiles.

Then things had not gone as planned. The two French patriots who should have been at the arranged rendezvous were not there. So the S.B.S team had moved with extra stealth through the dangerous darkness of this French countryside which was so strongly fortified and garrisoned by the Germans until they reached the comparative safety of this coppice of dense shrubs and thin trees. They would rest here all day and travel again tonight.

Crouching beside Lieutenant Brown, the commander of this S.B.S team, Bill Wainwright loudly and authoritatively ordered, 'Wake up, lieutenant!'

The young officer and the other three S.B.S. sailors immediately reacted to Bill's command. These tremendously well trained, exceptionally experienced men almost instinctively leapt from deep refreshing sleep to alert military readiness. Each man grabbed the loaded Sten-gun lying at his side and held it in hair-triggered alertness.

'Relax lads,' Bill reassured them, 'there's no sudden danger.'
Still alert, all four stood silently questioningly staring at Bill, but no questions were asked. They knew he would quickly explain why he had wakened them.

He did. He pointed, 'There's some very interesting, very unusual activity going on at that road over there. I knew you would all want to see it.' He handed his sentry's binoculars to Lt Brown.

Petty Officer Tom Walker already had his binoculars at his eyes. For some time the lieutenant and the petty officer stood silently searching through their powerful lenses.

Lowering his binoculars, Lt Brown asked, 'Well, Tom, what do you make of that gathering of high ranking Jerries? Do you recognize any of them?'

The Petty Officer's reply was un-typically hesitant and uncertain. 'It... It seems impossible, but one of these Jerries looks like - very like - Hitler. In fact I.. I think he really is Adolf Bloody Hitler!'

Lt. Brown nodded, but said nothing. He turned to leading seaman Wainwright , 'What do you think, Bill? You keenly observed them before you woke us, didn't you?'

'Aye I did. I agree with Tom. I'm sure it *is* Hitler over there. And I think two of those Jerries "top-brass" with him are Field Marshals Rommel and von Rundstedt.'

'Yes, that's what I think. Three perfect targets for us to "take out" eh, lads?' The Lieutenant's team nodded and smiled. Had it been even remotely possible for them to do so, none of them would have hesitated to risk their own lives in an attempt to kill Hitler and two of his top army officers. But these five S.B.S experts in eliminating important targets (although they had failed in their attempt to kill Field Marshal Rommel in France before D-Day)knew that such a mission was utterly impossible with the weapons they were armed with today.

Lt. Brown voiced all their thoughts as he sighed, 'Oh for sniper's rifle!' Petty Officer Walker echoed that sigh, 'Aye, if we had a couple of our sniper's rifles with us we could "eliminate" those three Jerry bastards. And if we killed Hitler surely this bloody war would end.'

All these S.B.S sailors had been expertly scrutinizing the land between them and the road where Hitler and his senior officers were grouped around their parked staff cars. If only they had been armed with snipers's rifle they would have left this coppice and tried to get within range of these Germans. But, armed only with sub-machine guns and automatic pistols, it would impossible to get past the many guarding German soldiers and to bring these weapons within range of those prime targets.

Lt. Brown again sighed, then again said, 'Oh for a sniper's rifle! From along that hedge there Hitler would be just about in range - extreme range- of our special, high-velocity sniper's bullets. However, unfortunately, that's not to be.'

Some five minutes later, amongst a flurry of stiff - armed Nazi salutes, Hitler got into his staff car. It accelerated eastwards towards the airfield where his special Luftwaffe aircraft was waiting ready to speed him back to Berlin.

The other staff cars took the two German Field Marshals westward to the forward headquarters from which they were directing their army's attacks against what was, even at this late date, the 17th June, 1944, the still somewhat precarious British beach-head in Normandy. It was ironic that it was from these same headquarters that these same officers had expected in 1940 to help direct "Operation Sealion" - the German invasion of England.

Lieutenant Brown smiled, 'Well, lads, it looks as if that's the show over. Its a sight I would have hated to miss. Thanks for waking us up to see it, Bill.'

Bill grinned, 'In years to come we'll be telling our children and grandchildren about this, won't we? The amazing fact that during the war we actually saw Adolf Hitler.'

Although his four comrades smiled and nodded their agreement, each man's unspoken thoughts were the same: 'Will I survive this bloody war? Will I live to father children to tell this story to?'

★ ★ ★

Two days later all these S.B.S. men were safely back in England.

Commander Richardson, the Royal Navy intelligence officer debriefing Lt. Brown, said, 'Well, lieutenant, I think that's about everything. You and your team have again done a brilliant job of destroying these flying-bombs.' The Commander grinned, 'And I can confirm that what you reported was correct. That *was* Adolf Hitler you saw! He *did* fly into France that day to confer with Rommel and von Rundstedt. Unfortunately we didn't learn this until too late, otherwise the R.A.F. would have tried to shoot down his plane or have tried to kill him in his staff car.'

'Yes, sir, and it was also most unfortunate that on that mission my S.B.S team were not armed with sniper's rifles.'

'Yes, Hitler certainly took quite a risk that day. He was very lucky not to killed by your team or by the R.A.F.' Commander Richardson thoughtfully paused then, almost as if talking to himself, murmured, 'Was it just luck that saved Hitler that day, or was some higher power, some strange, perverse God looking after him?'

★ ★ ★

Slightly more than one month later Commander Richardson was again, but more forcefully, more insistently, asking himself that question: 'Was some strange God perversely looking after Hitler?' The more he thought about it, the more likely this seemed.

Not only had Hitler safety - and it seemed bravely, for he had been awarded an iron cross- come through the horrors of the trenches of the First World War when millions of better men had savagely died, but he had successfully evaded R.A.F fighters on that day when he flew into France, and only the lack of a sniper's rifle saved him from falling victim to that S.B.S team that same day.

And now, to crown all that, Hitler has survived the German Army Officers bomb plot to kill him. The attaché case containing the plotters bomb had been correctly placed beside Hitler as he stood at the map table in his Rastenburg headquarters in East Germany, but then, just before the bomb exploded, he had suddenly moved to the opposite side of the table. That large, solid oak map table shielded Hitler from the explosion that killed four officers who had remained where he had been standing a few moments ago.

So once again Hitler escaped death.

And so once again Commander Richardson pondered that question: 'Has some higher power - some Fate, or destiny, or God - once more miraculously saved Hitler? Or was it just pure blind chance that saved him?'

Thinking of the many times he had stood to attention and sang the British national anthem, the Commander wondered could it possibly be that the God who does save our Gracious King also saves Hitler?.... perversely saves that evil monster and allows him to continue this terrible war and condemn many more to violent deaths?

Commander Richardson wearily sighed... No Religion, no Philosophy seemed to have a satisfactory answer to the problem of why a compassionate loving God allowed Evil to thrive.

Grim Harvest
(Germany, 1945)

Slithering painfully slowly this British troop train snails
ever deeper into war-devastated defeated Germany
on war-wrecked, not yet fully repaired rails.
As they slide mile after desolate mile, British soldiers,
battle-hardened veterans and inexperienced young rookies alike,
stare with almost unbelieving awe at all they saw.
Every further revelation of another Dante-demented city
brings deeper sadness, darker despair as young, emotional,
inexperienced British voices express their profound sorrow,
their heart-felt pity for this defeated country's
utter devastation, its countless civilian deaths.
Older, battle-scarred, be-ribboned veterans get annoyed,
angrily raise their voices: 'Oh, you damned ignorant
virgin milksops, hold your breath!
These bloody Jerries only got what they deserved!
These self-same Jerries wildly applauded when their
glorious Luftwaffe was bombing and devastating
other countries!'

Admonished and abashed, these now freshly thoughtful young
rookies knew that what these veterans so forcefully said
was all too true.
They thought of some of these Luftwaffe victims:
Warsaw, Rotterdam, London, Coventry, Clydebank;
certainly no Germans, military or civilians, had ever shrank
from loud applause and wholehearted praise
for those brave Luftwaffe bomber boys.
Yes, these young rookies wisely decided, the guilt,
the responsibility, is all the Germans own,
they had only reaped the terrible grim harvest
that they themselves had sown!

Hitler Youth
(Germany, December 1945)

These marauding Nazi 'Werewolves' are fiercer than real wolves;
these fanatic Hitler Youths are lead by tough, battle-hardened,
fugitive S.S. veterans who attack and kill and steal
then retreat to their concealing woods
where they hide and evade the waiting noose.

Late that freezing night British sentries are alerted
by sudden shots, then they vaguely see shadowy movements
that might be made by deadly stealthy 'Werewolves'.
There are strange, snow-muffled sounds,
there are confused voices that violently curse
in English and German.
There are many flashing, clattering sub-machine guns firing
and inaccurately scattering their deadly vicious burst.

Now comes that long cold wait through the now silent night
and then with dawn's growing light comes the cautious scouting.
We are told that two of our comrades have been carried away...
Wounded or dead?..none can say.
We find one body, a German youth,
one who had been a deadly dangerous Hitler Youth.
His right hand still clutched his gun,
we try to strip that weapon from him
but these stark allies, frost and death
hold it in their vice-like tenacious grip
that welds stiff fingers to freezing steel.

Those blue Teutonic eyes which had blazed such fanatic hate,
that had refused to believe Hitler was dead,
are now death-dimmed, are now ice-rimmed with frozen tears,
and, as they so blankly stare, they still seem to display
that misguided youth's terrible last fears.

Echoing out from beyond his grave the Führer's voice
still reached some, is still believed as it distorts truth
and screams vile, evil, lies
and now it had reached out and had claimed
yet one more sadly deluded, evily indoctrinated Hitler Youth.

The Chosen
(A Story)

Once again that young British soldier cursed the military police. When least wanted, the army's own policemen would be sure to turn up; but now when they *were* wanted there was no sign of them.

For almost forty minutes he had been waiting here, sitting alone in the cab of this motionless army lorry and still there were no sign of the armed military police who were to escort him on his journey to the British army barracks fifteen miles west of Hamburg.

Despite the wool-lined leather jerkin over his khaki uniform he was getting very cold sitting in this un-heated lorry. He gazed forlornly out at the deserted, freezing, snow-shrouded scene stretching all around him. He again re-assured himself that this was the correct rendezvous point where he had been instructed to wait for his armed escort. Again he angrily cursed the non-appearance of the military police: 'Another complete shambles.. another typical army balls-up!'

It was mid-December of 1945 and the severe winter was inflicting its torture over this dismal post-war German landscape. A vast snowy sea of undulating waves completely submerged Hamburg's endless heaps of rubble. Many of these drifts were more than thirty feet deep. Only hundreds of stark walls, the shells of gutted buildings, rising like giants tombstones over the graveyard of this once thriving city revealed the extent of its overwhelming devastation.

The young soldier shuddered with cold and dismay as he surveyed that desolate scene. Again his eyes were drawn towards the fantastically contorted sculptures of twisted girders rising above the banks of the frozen River Elbe and marking the site of a ruined shipyard. But still there was no sign of those missing British military policemen anywhere in all this vast, depressing white waste,

He decided to wait no longer. He would make the potentially dangerous journey on his own.

His lorry was laden with food for his British army barracks. Driving over the fifteen miles of icy roads to that military base would be hazardous enough, but a greater hazard threatened in the dark fir forests which stretched on both sides of much of the road. Skulking in these forest were packs of 'Werewolves'. These packs consisted of heavily armed groups of Hitler Youths led by fugitive S.S. soldiers. They were all fanatic Nazis who refused to believe that their revered Führer was dead. True to the 'Werewolf' symbols they defiantly painted on walls, these ferocious predators left the shelter of the forest at night and raided British army bases for food and other supplies.

Driven desperate by cold and hunger they had started ambushing British lorries in daylight. They had killed four British soldiers on this road. Each lorry was now supposed to have a well armed military police escort.

The young soldier grimly thought, 'Maybe I've got no bloody 'redcap' escort, but at least I'm not completely un armed.'

He reached down and patted the reassuring bulge of the loaded revolver in the web holster at his right hip.

Gently he eased the lorry onto the icy road and cautiously started his journey. As he was leaving the outskirts of Hamburg and was attempting to negotiate a sharp bend the lorry went into a slow, irrecoverable skid on the treacherous ice. It slithered off the road, slid down a smooth slope, then dug itself into a deep snowdrift.

Looming darkly against the bright snow, strange figures mysteriously appeared. Wrapped in bulky layers of clothing these shapeless creatures hardly seemed human as they emerged from their underground lairs.

Stumbling, falling, and rising, they slowly but resolutely forced their way through the obstructing snow. Behind these six or seven creatures came about a dozen children who desperately struggled to keep up with the adults. All were urgently homing in on the food spilled from the stranded British army lorry.

Starvation makes all creatures cruel and selfish. None of these almost starving refugees had compassion to spare for the dazed British soldier who sprawled motionless in the lorry's cab.

The only concern of these desperately hungry refugee mothers was to get food for their weak, malnourished, skeleton thin children and themselves. With trembling urgency they started digging in the snow for that spilled food.

Suddenly a commanding, menacing, Teutonic voice roared out, 'Drop that food! Get back to your rat-holes and starve, you Jews. You filthy Jewish rats.' A seventeen year old German youth – a fanatic Hitler Youth – stood behind them. He held a Lüger pistol in one hand. He pointed at the oldest Jew who shuffled forward and placed himself in front of the cowering women and petrified children. Despite his stooped, narrow shouldered frail appearance that white bearded Patriarch radiated defiant dignity as he unflinchingly faced the young German.

The Hitler Youth – that perfect, blonde haired, blue eyes specimen of 'The Master Race'– took careful aim at the ancient Jew – that perfect specimen of 'God's Chosen People.'

Suddenly the young Nazi trembled violently... trembled with overwhelming hate. He grasped the pistol with both hands to steady it as his finger tightened on the trigger.

Desperate mothers clutched whimpering children. They closed their eyes.

They urgently prayed.

A single shot blasted out.

It echoed over the desolate landscape. It flung hungry crows into startled – but hopeful–cawing flight.

When the cowering Jewish women forced themselves to open their eyes they were astounded to see their Patriarch still alive, still defiantly standing upright. They were even more amazed to see the body of the young Nazi lying motionless in the snow. Almost in disbelief they stared at his crumpled body and at the blood oozing from his back and vividly staining the snow.

The young British soldier appeared from behind the cab of the lorry. He held his revolver in his right hand. A wisp of bluish smoke rose from its barrel. He ploughed purposefully through the snow then stooped and removed the Lüger pistol from the cold hand of the dead young German. He then turned and smiled at the old Jew.

With a tremulous struggle the old man peeled layers of gloves off his right hand. He thrust it out. With surprising strength his emaciated fingers grasped the young soldier's firm hand, 'Thank you.... thank you. You save our life.'
The soldier grinned, 'You speak excellent English.'

Deeply caved in his gaunt pale face the old man's dark eyes gleamed with pride, 'I taught English at Warsaw University many, many years ago.'

'You are Polish?'

Pride again brightened his tired old eyes, 'Yes, yes, I am Polish. We are all Polish Jews. We are refugees from our poor, sad, devastated Poland. We manage to escape from Warsaw Ghetto.'

The British soldier nodded sympathetically. He knew how Warsaw had suffered; how much of it had been systematically razed to the ground by the Germans. He asked, 'How long have you been refugees?'

'For too long... oh, for much too long'

The soldier was surprised to see a grin appear on that gaunt, ravished old face. The grin spread. It wonderfully animated and radiated his entire countenance as the old Jew continued, 'We, our poor Jewish people, are refugees - are wanderers - for two thousand years!'

He straightened himself, he held his head high, with passionate certainly he declared, 'But soon now we have our own country. Soon we have our new - our ancient - country. That is where we go, to re-born Israel!'

The soldier nodded in agreement, 'Yes I'm sure you will get to your own country soon.' 'Noticing that the women and children were standing and staring uncertainly he said, 'Tell them to help themselves to the food; there's plenty for us all.'

'Thank you.. thank you. You are most good.'

While the women and children urgently gathered food the old man stared at the young British soldier; he arranged his thoughts into English then said, 'I hope you do not mind what I say... I have much surprise at you. Most British soldiers are too - soft?- yes, too soft with the Germans ... those terrible Germans, but not you. You kill that young Nazi with no mercy. You do good... much good, but still I have much surprise. You understand?'

'Oh yes I understand your surprise.' He grinned, 'But I had little choice, did I? If I hadn't ruthlessly killed him, he would have killed you, wouldn't he?

'Yes, yes of course that is true.'

The young soldier again grinned, 'But what you say is true. Many British soldiers *are* too soft with the Germans. Probably I was a bit too soft myself. During the war I never liked killing Germans even though they were trying to kill me. Whenever possible I tried to take German soldiers prisoner instead of killing them. But I learned. I'm different now.'

'Oh, that is true. You do not mind killing that young Nazi.' The old Jew stared enquiringly, 'Why?... Why you not soft now?'

The young soldier hesitated; hideous vivid memories flooded his mind. He grimaced then solemnly explained, 'Near the end of the war I was amongst the first British soldiers to enter and liberate Belsen Concentration Camp. After all the horrors I saw there I no longer tried to take any German soldiers prisoners . After that I had absolutely no compunction about killing Germans.'

The old Polish Jew nodded his profound understanding. He reached out and again firmly grasped the young British soldier's hand with both of his. With a trembling voice he exclaimed, 'Ah yes, I understand.'

For long silent moments the old man and the young soldier stared into one another's eyes. Then the old man sighed. He sighed as sadly, as movingly, as only an old Jew can sigh; one who, homeless and dispossessed, is war-weary, is world weary; one who has seen his wife and children brutally killed; has seen so many sent to slave labour and to the gas chambers.

He shuddered then gently, with infinite compassion, murmured, 'Ah yes, I understand...I understand! Belsen... Belsen. Terrible!...Terrible!'

The Cobbler

The Cobbler – that triple – peaked 'Jewel in the crown
of the Arrochar Alps' – is where generations of Glasgow's
best youths have eagerly discovered what the hill have to give.
There they honed their rock climbing skills;
there they learned the comradeship of high camping;
there learned what it is to truly live.

Weekend after weekend, laden with heavy rucksack,
they make that long steep climb up from Arrochar's salty shore;
they repeat their easy scrambles on grey old Cobbler's Central peak.
Freely scrambling and clambering they get to know
and get to love these Glasgow – handy Arrochar Hills.
These keen young novice climbers are almost awed to meet
and greet some noble older climbers; those already almost
legendary 'old-timers' who had, by their inspiring example,
guided some of Glasgow's young unemployed, pre-war
working class to delight in the immense thrills
to be found on Scotland's challenging summer and winter hills.
There was sturdy Tom Weir, always clad in his cosy
wooly hat; there was Jock Nimlin with his named
Cobbler rock-route; there was old Ben Humble, completely
deaf, but completely undaunted.
Haunted by memories of these living legends, keen youngsters
soon disdain the too easy Central Peak,
they hurry with youthful restlessness to seek
the Cobbler's daunting South Peak.
They soon become familiar with its well-used,
well-loved climbs, all clearly marked by the white scrapes
of past generations savagely nailed climbing boots.

They then go on to test their nerves on the Cobbler's North Peak,
on its much newer, much more severe rock routes
where even bold youth is at times touched with fear.
With neat new light boots precariously poised
on an airy one inch edge,
with nerves and muscles under immense strain,
they inwardly assure themselves (and how they hope it's true)
that they are as safe and secure as on two foot ledge!
Yes, here they truly lived. For these true golden, well-filled years
they are wondrously alive...
had gloriously lived nearer to how Nature intended!

Red Deer Stags

Rock Climbing

Glorious are those sun blessed days
when we escape the city's mundane ways;
as eager feet stride fresh heights
we rejoiced in Summers pulsing light.

No longer petty creatures with paltry hopes,
our spirits soar as eager fingers secure our climbing ropes,
we become bright creatures with giant secret fears
as that inspiring, and daunting, mountain rears.

Beneath the hand there's the feel of sun-warmed rock
and a silence wiser than all man's talk,
we make sure movements of foot and hand....
Life is here ... and Life is Grand!

The New Foreman

As he collected his pay, the shipyard manager told him
he was now promoted foreman;
told him he must go to Dunn's the Hatter's and buy his
foreman's special bowler hat the very next day.
That reinforced bowler was not merely a trapping of power,
a head-swelling badge of rank,
without the protection of their special bowlers there were parts
of Fairfield Shipyard from which management shrank.
Accidents will happen, but it was odd how often
red-hot rivets were 'accidentally' dropped from high
when unpopular managers or foremen happened to be passing by!

On Monday morning the new foreman, from habit, puts on
his auld grey bonnet, then remembering, takes down his
brand-new special bowler, almost shyly, almost reluctantly,
he dons it.
His wife peers from behind curtains as he leaves their tenement,
she's proud of that bowler and of her man,
now all the neighbours (especially that snooty lot upstairs)
will ken her braw, burly husband has been promoted foreman.

His new bowler is greeted by workmates, is greeted with friendly
cheers
and with some not so friendly jeers.
Their new foreman promises that, this evening in their favourite
pub on pub-crowded Govan Road, he will stand them all
free beers; meanwhile those who are not too embittered
and indoctrinated modern 'Red Clydesiders' laughingly serenade him
with a mocking song to the tune of 'The Red Flag':
'We, the working class must now kiss your arse
now that you've got the Foreman's job at last!'

Then, in a somewhat reluctant, somewhat desultory way
they get down to work, down to earning their pay.
Slowly - all too slowly - new ships rise on impatient waiting slipways
to the sound of the riveters hammering din,
that productive noise that is all too often stilled
by all too many self-destructive un-official strikes.

As these Clydeside shipyard workers thoughtless revel
in this post-war shipbuilding boom they increasingly praise
their world-famous Clyde Built Ships, praise them to the skies.
But the new foreman has secret fears;
He knows these ships are costed at an inflated rate,
are all too often delivered all too late.
He worries how long can this continue, this never meeting
scheduled delivery dates?
How will our shipyards manage to complete and survive
once our War-time enemies become our Peace-time competitors?
How many more years before the first Clydeside shipyards dies?

Climbing Companions

Where, except in war's hellish brew,
does one gain such true friends?...
Friends who, the greatest of climbing buddies,
rejoice in sharing their highest mountain delights,
who, awed, shared one another's near fatal climbing frights..

Great is the glowing joy these climbing companions know
when the leading climber is up
and this new snow and ice route will 'go'.
Then how immense is the summit gained thrill
of seeing so many, as yet unclimbed, Highland hills
stretching seeming endless in the proud display
of the clear purity of their virgin snow.

Then later there's all that cheery chat,
all those old, oft-told, hilarious stories,
all the laughter, then the loud chorus
round the winter camp-fires blazing glory
where outstretched hands and stockinged feet
slowly, pleasantly, roast while each wind-chilled
back shivers and freezes.

These climbing companions also share the unbelievable glory
of sweltering August days when mountain distances
are deceptively misted by clinging layers of hazy heat,
and, gloriously active, they sweatily use
and hopefully improve, their rock-climbing skills
until even the most keen of novice youngsters are beat
by the unrelenting fierceness of this sweaty summer heat.
They are tempted by another of their Highland hills
many deceptive tricks as a high, modest, mountain lochan
glittery lures and mischievously conceals its true temperature

with its shimmering, alluring, Mediterranean blue.
How eagerly each climber takes his turn to plunge...
how terrible is that breath-snatching, heart stopping shock
as that deceptive lochan reveals its true Arctic chill.
Gasping, shouting, laughing, they try to convince themselves
they are honestly enjoying yet another glorious mountain thrill
in their beloved Scottish hills.

And yet, despite that lochan's cruel deceptive chill,
despite the worst of some summer's rains and gales
and the most atrocious of some winter's blinding blizzards
that their Scottish hills can - and do - fling at them
these climbing companions have gained vast rewards,
have forged their greatest, life-long friendships,
have stored a mountainous hoard of mountains memories.
They shuddery remember mountain days that were profoundly physical;
then there were other memorable times that were sublimely spiritual;
truly were almost awesomely mystical.

When meeting together at relaxed ease all these
climbing companions wholeheartedly agree with William Blake...
When receptive men and inspiring mountains meet
most wondrous powerful things can be done....
Things that most certainly 'are not done by crowds jostling in the street.'

Couthie Youth Hostel

Late arrived winter climbers fling wide the Youth Hostel's door,
admit a blast of fierce blizzards as they, and it, wildly storm in;
stamp clinging snow from clumsy boots,
shower powdery snow from cowling hoods,
eagerly greet hostel's blast of fuggy air.
From crowded common-room's vivacious noise
a convivial voice declares:
'Och, you would think it was snowing oot there.'

Armed with alarmingly large frying-pans, hostellers jostle
for precious space around huge cast-iron cooking-stove;
in places that stove glows red-hot;
weather beaten sweaty faces glow almost as hot.
Mouth-watering bacon cheerily sizzles,
jolly fat bangers spluttery giggle,
black-puddings - innocently unaware of cholesterol's dangers-
greedily soak up tasty animal fats.

Above that stove, on crowded pulley and sagging ropes,
saturated clothes gently steam and steadily drip;
some drips drop into cooking-pots,
maybe these drips give an extra flavour
to hardly old hosteller's uniquely tasty gravy!

Huge kettles steamily hiss and cheerily rattle lids;
a novice winter climber, an apprentice Clydeside engineer,
revelling in all this hissing bliss, laughs:
'Och, that's a richt braw noise...

A truly Watt-inspiring steamy noise.'
He then gets on with the more immediate bliss
of his hardy, hardly cordon bleu cooking.

Snuggly seated around well scrubbed tables
hostellers from all walks of life convivially meet;
some wolfish eat, some burply replete, have eaten.
Lusty singers join in as mouth-organs gustily repeat
summers boisterous camp-fire songs.

An ultra-vivacious young English lady climber brightly asks:
'Who's game to go out and make a jolly big snowman?'
None seem too keen.
In uncertain silence all clearly hear the baffled blizzard
batter the hostels windows and stout old walls
like a drunken lout furious at being kept out.

An auld, white-bearded 'worthie' - a retired postman,
a non-retired poacher - who's been imbibing something
suspiciously illicitly alcoholic,
empathically replies in broadest Doric:
'Och, lass, ho'd yer haivers.. awa tae buggery
wi' gaein oot in that,
we'll a' stay richt cosy here in this couthie wee hostels
brawly fuggy snuggery!'

Highland Woods

Walking in Highland Woods I saw a forester
hammer in a post at that river down below...
The sound carried clear, each hefty hammer blow.

I watch the heavy hammer rise and fall,
each loud thump occurs when it's poised above his head...
'not so!' my reason said.

The I saw a warning notice set upside down;
twisting my head, I read – topsy – turvy spelling-
'Danger, tree felling!'

Smiling I thought, 'Thank God for Highland Woods
where individuality is not yet dead,
where strict regulations are still set upon their head!'

Glasgow Trams

Shopping laden, the auld Glasgow housewife struggles
on to a familiar Glasgow tram.
The young Pakistani conductor helps her to a seat.
She profusely thanks him, the first coloured conductor
she has met, she thinks him most pleasant,
most tidy and neat, so full of youthful slim grace.
His teeth gleam bright in that smiling brown face
beneath that large white turban on his head.

The auld wifie thinks this Paki is much nicer than some
o' yon Glasgow conductresses; some are real impatient
soor-faced bitches!
Och, but in fairness, most wur guid natured craturs
aye ready wi' a laugh even when maist harassed
on overcrowded platform, geing their favourite cry of:
'Com on - get aff!'
The old tram sped rattling and staggering, its bell clanging,
through those endless, dull, grim grey tenemented
Glasgow streets as cheerily warm-heartedly noisy
as a pay-day Glesga drunk singing his homeward way
on happily staggering uncertain feet.

Sitting quietly contentedly, pleased with the familiar
passing scene, the auld wifie idly wonders how Glaswegians
would ever manage without their guid auld tram caurs;
these trams that boast different braw colours on every one
of the many routes that criss-cross this sprawling vivacious city.
'Aye, it wad be a awfa pity if we ever lost oor braw caurs!'

In rare, precious, summer sunshine these tram wear
a swaggering jaunty air,
and, bravely brawly speeding, fair shoogle passengers
descending their narrow twisting stairs.
Then, during the worst, most miserable, almost un-penetrable
pea-souper of a December fog when all other transport
gets hopelessly lost or does not dare venture abroad,
these faithful auld Glesca caurs gamely battle on,
and, always gloriously victorious, doggedly win through.

The auld Glesca wifie arrives at her destination
and the friendly Pakistani conductor helps her off
then hands down her heavy laden shopping bags.
She smiles her thanks, 'Ta, son, yuir awfa kind helping me doon.'
Then, with a sympathetic glance at his white turbaned –
but what she thinks is his thickly bandaged-head,
she murmurs to herself, 'Aw the poor wee soul,'
then loudly, sincerely, compassionately, said,
'An, son, a' hope yuir sair heid gets better soon!'

Rannoch Railway Bothy

From Kingshouse we - the young, eager, three of us- set out
to cross from West to East on the obscure tracks across
the desolate peat-hagged vastness of Rannoch Moor.
Before long we're cursing and stumbling as we negotiate
our precarious way past what seems endless weary miles
of peat-black bottomless bogs where what seems
the semi-fossilized remnants of the ancient Caledonian Forest
reach out from that preserving peat like haggish witches who
sinister beckon , or try to snatch and claw
with peat splattered splintered fingers,
or like some slimy pre-historic monsters who scarily
reach out with long, scaly, peat black claws.

But all too soon we face a much more real threat of death
than those half-imaged dark dangers as a savage blizzard
sudden slashes in from the East.
With gasping urgency we press on into that fierce storm that,
getting ever fiercer, threatens to smother man and beast.

Now we're in real trouble; we halt, we consult;
should we press on?.. should we turn back?
If we try to return to distant Kingshouse this blizzard
will be battering our backs, will not be slashing into our faces,
but - perhaps youthfully foolishly we're most loath
to ignominiously turn back....
We unanimously decide to push on.
We're guided by one visionary image that keeps us going
as this fiendish blizzard increases its fury...
We brightly visualize a real cosy wee railway bothy
beside that Rannoch railway track
that stretches unseen somewhere Eastward before us.

At last, at long, long last, exhausted, almost at our last gasp
we quite literally, and profoundly thankfully, stumble over that
snow-smoothed Rannoch railway track.
Now which way to the nearest, desperately needed railway bothy?
Turning South, we human snow-ploughs force our weary way
along those snow-hidden rails and urgent search through
whirling snow's blinding white
and descending dusk's rapid dimming light.

Threatened despair turns to vast relief as a neat wee bothy looms
through the miserable shrouding gloom.
Freezing fingers light candles; an urgent shovel uncovers
a glorious heap of railway coals.
Soon a roaring fire cheers us..
Cheers and heats and soars our rejoicing souls.

We're profoundly thankful that steam trains still ply
this West Highland route...
good old steam engines, coal-guzzlers that proudly, loudly,
nonchalantly belch out vast clouds of steam, smoke, and soot.
We hurriedly change into blissfully dry clothes
and, basking in the wee iron stoves red-hot glow,
we scorn the howling storms demented snow.
As our soaking clothes hang and drip and steam, the atmosphere
gets as fuggily cosily cheery as a Glasgow wash-house steamy.
We eat, we drink, we are happy, sleepy, dreamy.

With nostalgic thanks we praises these great Victorian engineers
who undaunted struggled on with this forever sinking
Rannoch railway line and who, at last, floated it on a vast
lengthy raft of countless trees that to this present day
enable steam trains to pass along soggily boggy Rannoch Moor's
Eastern edge with consummate ease.

As generous drams revive and enliven us our spirits soar,
shared memories again flow, happy old tales are re-told;
with heedless abandon we heap more and yet more illicit
railway coals into our gregarious roaring furnace- hot stove.
Unanimously we whole - heartedly agree that we
would not exchange our humble wee bothy's cosy bliss
for any luxurious Savoy or Ritz..
pampered luxury can not beat this!

Auld Scots Pines

How grand that – against daunting odds – some magnificent
remnants of the Ancient Caledonian Forest still stand;
defiant clinging on have survived the worst excesses
of successive centuries; have even come through the
life and timber devouring miseries of the First
and Second World Wars.

The most sturdy of these rugged auld Scots Pines
seem 'half as old as Time;' they live on, the tattered survivors
of a vanquished army that hide away in some of the
Highlands most isolated, most beautiful locations.
Winning their courageous struggle through Highland history
these ancient trees continue to enhance
the enchanting wonders of Loch Maree;
defying sly encroaching Hydro–dams, they survive,
they even thrive, in the noble glory of Glen Cannich;
by displaying the grandness that is the Rothiemurchus Forest
they ease the stark harshness of the vast Cairngorms.
They cling with determined strength to their
most Southerly bastion –
the lovely, lonely, Black Woods of Rannoch.

To visit these scattered remnants and gaze with visionary eyes
is to see how Scotland's Highlands landscape used to be.
No two of these magnificent rugged trees are quite alike;
each time – battered Pine gives a unique erratic display
of storm – contorted limbs,
and each tree flys its highest, proudest, bottle-green banners
that defy the worst that time and winter weather can fling.

We must ensure these ancient trees suffer no further decline;
we must see that those noble stands of Scots Pines
continue to give their vibrant aesthetic pleasure,
remain for ever part of our country's National Treasure.
As they withstand the worst ravages of Nature and of Man
perhaps in time, perhaps in an again Independent Scotland,
future generations may rejoice to see much of the Highlands again
nobly clad in these fine auld Scots Pines.

Winter Camping

(Things are done when men and mountains meet,
things that are not done by crowds jostling in the street)
                                    William Blake.

Our small, yellow, candle-lit tent is a strange solitary dot,
a pale pin-point of light that sheds a faint orange glow
that's almost lost amongst the vast winter snows
of this high Cairngorm Plateau.
As 'snug as bugs,' we luxuriate in our first post-war luxury,
our genuine Norwegian eider-down sleeping-bags that we've long
longed for, and long saved for.
As we appreciatively sip our savagely hot, rum-fortified tea
we joyously re-live today's wondrous strenuous
hours of skilful climbing on ice and snow.

As we think about settling down for the night we become
ever more aware of the strange powerful pull of midnight's full moon.
We agree it would be quite mad to leave our snug sleeping-bags
and our cosy wee tent at this haunting hour,
but then we also quickly agree, 'Sure it would be madness,
but surely be a wise, attractive, full moon inspired madness.'
The entire Cairngorm Plateau is a wonderland of pure
windless silence and the endless silver glitter of moon-glow snow.
Prominent rounded knolls seem strange, stranded, monstrous whales
left over from the last Ice Age.
We cautiously walk, we often stop, we hardly talk,
stilled in breathless wonder we seem to gaze
through endless time and through limitless space.

Then as mountain frost ever more keenly increases its
tenacious grip our shivering flesh brings us back to mundane earth
and suddenly our snuggly luxurious Norwegian sleeping-bags
seem ever more wondrously alluring.
Revelling in the crisp crunch of our boots on frost crystallized snow
we head for our cosy wee tent's cheery beckoning orange glow.

Again as 'snug as bugs' in our sleeping-bags,
again fortified and perhaps made wise by more rum-laced tea,
we try to analyse what we have magically –
or even mystically? – felt tonight.
Are there some real, profound, deep hidden meanings to be found
in the wondrous beauty of this high, snow-smothered,
moon-gleaming Cairngorm Plateau?...
Things that, like Blake's 'crowds jostling in the street,'
most humans can never hope to know?

Perhaps, thanks to our glorious glowing remembrance
of today's strenuous snow and ice climbing successes
and then tonight's huge, full-mooned, almost excessive
aesthetic pleasures – to say nothing of all those generous mugs
of rum-laced-tea we are now possessed by a rather heady
mixture of sensual and aesthetic delights.

After much profound, but not too drearily serious debate we
decide it's much wiser just to accept such disparate gifts
and not try to deeply analyse them, but just let them,
by complementing one another, increase the pleasure
we get from each one.
We drowsily think we've profoundly clever to arrive
at this wise philosophy.
We also quickly agree that if some religious beliefs
might be needed to go with tonight's spiritual, aesthetic,
even mystic (?) delights, our own beliefs
will not be anything dully dourly Calvanistic,
will rather be something primitively paganly Pantheistic,
our own special God will probably be rascally old Bacchus
with His faith that's openly unashamedly Hedonistic.

Vivid Contrasts

Standing on Ben Lomond's snow-pure summit we gaze in awe;
the sky is an endless glow of cloudless eggshell blue,
to North and West there limitless spreads
a panoramic glory of snow-bright mountain views.
But not quite all we see is endlessly uplifting,
for to the South East is a sight to appal.
Clear seen from Glasgow's favourite hill is a widespread
dark grey smudge that is Glasgow's funereal foggy pall
that's suicidally inflicted on that city by its all too many
chimneys belching out their all too deadly filthy coal smoke.
We resolutely refuse to let the awful thought of returning
tonight to that filthy foggy city's dismal misery
spoil today's sun and snow bright uplifting glory.

That evening, passing in our Glasgow bound bus, it seems that
even the castle-crowned solidity of Dumbarton Rock
has been foggily vagued away.
At Clydebank we do manage see the gaunt grey walls
of roofless tenements, all stark reminders of the
Luftwaffe's devastating Blitz.
As the Clyde - Glasgow's own, much loved, much polluted river-
gets ever narrower Glasgow's own, much feared fog, gets ever thicker,
ever filthier, and our bus crawls ever slowest along beside
the foggy pall of the unseen tidal Clyde
then through what seems the fog-increased vastness
of Glasgow's ugly urban sprawl.

At last we leave our hour's late bus and, almost braille-like,
vaguely grope our homeward way through traffic-less,
and even fog-defeated tram-less streets.
With weeping eyes increasing smarting,
and labouring lungs increasing gasping,
we endure the final miles through what is no mere common fog
but is now a deadly killer smog...
A new, man-made plague, a Devilish evil black Death
that condemns many in this poor old city to an early
ugly, phlegm coughing bronchial death.
The few pedestrians who have foolishly ventured out loom
with menacing suddenness from the shrouding gloom,
they vaguely gape then nervous hurry from our awful,
rucksack hunchbacked Hyde-like shapes.

As, smog-blinded, we hesitantly walk and stumble on
we manage to stoically talk....
We vividly remember our wondrous day on Ben Lomond,
we compare the delights of shining sun and glittering snow
with the despicable noxious filth of this smog-bound city...
It is like contrasting brightest day with darkest blight.
We wholehearted agree that we must – we indisputably will –
get out this sprawling city's soul-sapping misery,
will leave this city forever, will live a truer life
amongst our inspiring Highland Hills...
there perhaps in time we'll acquire some wholesome wisdom
from these ancient hills pre-history Pagan mystery.

PART TWO

Some Assynt Years

A Unique Chore

In those happy post-war years Scotland's Youth Hostels
were still *real* hostels where motor cars and motor-bikes
were strictly banned.
These hostels were only for the use of *real* hostellers –
keen active hikers, long-distant cyclists, daring mountain climbers,
and there were almost no showers or baths,
such things were considered foolish, foppish, sissy fads!

Each morning before going away on another happy, strenuous,
active day each hosteller was allocated a hostel cleaning chore;
some chores were easy, some were harder.
Learning that I was also a Youth Hostel Warden,
had spent one night at his huge, imposing, Carbrisdale Castle
hostel on route to open my small primitive, summer hostel
in West Sutherland, this massive hostel's smiling warden
kindly gave me a uniquely easy chore
before I left for Achmelvich's uniquely beautiful white shore.
Other hostellers, en route to clean some of this unique castle's
365 windows, or to scrub or mop some of its miles of wooden
or marble floors, smiled at me with jealous glee
as, armed with my long-handled feather duster,
I went about my uniquely easy chore of dusting
this hostel's many nude and near nude life-size marble statues.

A typically cheerily hardy wee Glasgow cyclist gave a
good-natural grumble, 'Och, laddie, that's a real braw chore
ye've got there. As for me, I'm awa tae once mair
clean some o' this castle awfa many marble lavvies.'
Wide grinning, he light-hearted added, 'An,' Jimmie,
mak' sure ye properly dust a' thae marble statue's
ticklish wee nooks an' crannies!'
So, conscientiously, but feeling increasingly foolish,
I continue my unique Youth Hostel chore
and felt ever more and more
light-headish, tickling-stickish Ken Doddish!

Highland Philosophy

As I share a leisurely Sabbath stroll with two local crofters
we - Donald Pollochan, Dougie Munro and me -
all halt, all again admire the familiar beauty of Achmelvich Bay;
this glorious view is wondrous enhanced,
its white sands given a shimmering glitter,
its clear waters emeralded a precious turquoise,
its deep seaweeds aquamarined an enchanting dark blue
by the pure translucent light of this perfect June day.

Drugged by all this breath-taking Beauty I quavery quote:
   'What is this life if, full of care,
   we have no time to stand and stare?'
Donald and Dougie together declare:
   'Och now, surely that is a poetic English prayer.'
Comfortably seating themselves on a convenient smooth rock
they playful grin and wisely enquire:
   'Why *stand* and stare when you can *sit* and stare?'
I also sit and wholehearted agree
with that wise, relaxed, Highland Philosophy of theirs.

Gone Fishing

Whenever Achmelvich Youth Hostel's warden was missing
and late arrived hostlers enquired about him
they were light-heartedly told:
'The warden's not here... he's gone fishing!'
This was not always quite true...
Sometimes he was to be seen on Achmelvich's
rabbit-infested sand dunes
keen shooting with his accurate Remington point two, two.

This shooting and fishing was not done just for fun;
the healthy, appetising, spoils of rod and gun
were real necessities to supplement the warden's
almost non-existent pay.
Without those generous spoils of the sea, of Assynt's many lochs,
and of Achmelvich's sand dunes, he would almost have starved.

Now, nostalgically looking back, the ex-warden laughed
as he remembered how, in these pre-indigestion day,
a large, old, iron frying-pan was his main cooking utensil;
how rarely the thick, dark brown fat was changed in that
wondrously greasy black frying-pan!
How gloriously the large, plump, fresh brown trout were fried,
how delightfully crispy crunchy were their skins,
how deliciously the tender pink flesh melted in his drooling mouth.
How immensely better they tasted than any supermarket's
frozen, neatly packed, plastic-wrapped apology for trout.

Oh yes, those were truly happy days...
Or do they seem such wondrous carefree times
just because they are now so very selectively remembered?
He now recalls that sometimes some hostlers got quite irate
at the warden being so often missing, being away fishing
when they urgent need food from the hostel's small shop.
Still, even the most irate of these hungry hostlers
were easily appeased, the warden's neglect of duty forgiven,
when they were given generous gifts of trout or haddock,
or even a tenderly plump, neatly gutted and skinned rabbit.
How these overjoyed hostlers then whole-hearted praised
the warden's gone shooting, gone fishing, habits!

Suilven

Some love Assynt's wild untamed landscape,
return to be renewed year after year.
Others visit only once, feel too uneasy
under Suilven's frowning stare,
feel some deep instinctive fear;
are awed by that dominating mountain
that's constantly crouching there.
When concealed in clouds it's still hunchback lurking,
patiently menacingly lurking...
a prehistoric monster malevolent in its lair!

Loch Roe Herring

Watching that graceful pleasure yacht
silent glide into the Admiralty charted
anchorage in Loch Roe, I think of past times
when that sheltered narrow loch
was crowded with sailing ships;
ships not gathered here for pleasure,
but to find profitable commercial treasure.

I shift my gaze to another place,
to the only flat land in all Ardroe's
heather-browned, peat-stained wildness;
a few acres that glow a verdant green,
made herring-gut lush by decades of Loch Roe's
highly prized 'Silver Darlings.'

From Achmelvich and Ardroe hardy crofters used to go
searching for herring in small, sturdy, heavy-oared boats;
they braved the worst the Minch could fling,
they brought back hardily gained high-heaped crans
that slithery overflowed when delivered
to anxious waiting daughters and wives
whose nimble fingers and keen gutting knives
became eye-defying blurs of motion.

Even these toil-hardened tough hands would painful sting
as they set layer after layer of gutted herring
in barrel after barrel then skilful fling in
handful after handful of coarse rock salt.
Row after regimented row of filled barrels
stood like proud, stout, barrel-chested soldiers
all patiently waiting to go
into gaping holds of impatient waiting sailing ships.

Not just British ships waited to fill their empty holds;
some sailed to Ardroe from Germany, Russia and Poland;
had been forced to venture further forth
when vast shoals of enigmatic herring
had suddenly, inexplicably, ceased to mass past
their own Baltic shores.
These Loch Roe herring had been – and,
according to local folk-lore – still were
much, much, better food;
still made a much more succulent meal
of salted herring and home-grown tatties
than any o' yon much more famous Loch Fyne herring ever could!

Poor Canisp

Once more I stare at that familiar pair, Canisp and Suilven,
once more I compare their companion shapes;
wryly smiling, I again feel sorry for Canisp,
poor, forever overshadowed Canisp, although you try
with utmost might, with your slightly higher height,
yet how can your more sedate smooth flowing
mellow sandstone slopes ever hope to compete
with flamboyant Suilven's sheer, upheaving,
domineering steep, with its awesome suggestion
of aeons of dramatic elemental powers?

Perhaps, wisely, you've long since ceased trying to compete,
perhaps you're resignedly content to play second fiddle,
be completely dominated by your awesome neighbour's
enigmatic sphinx-like riddle.

East Meets West

Only the warden, two female Edinburgh students
and an older, hardy, gregariously cheery
male Glasgow cyclist shared the comfort of
Achmelvich Youth Hostel's small common room.
All gloried in the wonder of this remote wee hostel's
cosy warmth; they delighted in the hot-glowing
pot-bellied iron stove that set the lids of huge kettles
cheerily steamily rattling as if mocking the fierce excesses
of the roaring Atlantic storm that kept the almost
horizontal rain almost incessant pouring.

Studiously immersed in serious books, these Edinburgh students
were quite a contrast to that rather rough, tough Glasgow cyclist,
that perfect example of Glasgow's unpretentious, unselfconscious
broad-spoken, but not un-read, working class.
The warden was secretly amused at this example
of East meeting West; of these snobbish members
of Morningside's middle-class best
trying not to mingle with that - as they thought -
rather uncouth Gorbals pest.
That cheery cyclist suddenly exclaimed, 'By God, I've got
a hell o' a drouth! I think I'll make a pot o' char.'
He winked at the warden then grinned at the students,
'Ye'll take a mug o' tea wi' us, won't you?
One students lifted her attractive, dark-haired head,
warily smiled, icily politely accepted his friendly offer.
The other kept her snooty nose deep buried in her book.

Undeterred by one's icy politeness, by the other's silent disdain
the cyclist tolerantly shrugged as he thought:
'After a' they're little mair than bairns!'
Cheerily he asked, 'An' whit are you studying hen?'
'Oh, I'm taking English Literature,' replied the nicer student.
Turning to the silent student the insistent Glaswegian then
forcefully asked, 'An' whit aboot you hen...
Whit are you studying?'
Asked point-blank, she could hardly continue silent reading;
she sighed, she raised haughty eyes, she gave an Arctic stare
then frostily said, 'Oh, really, if you must know,
actually I'm taking Medicine!'
Then disdainful eyes peevish droop to engrossing book.
Again the Glasgow cyclist tolerantly shrugged and thought:
'I dinna ken if you've a sair pain in yer belly...
But, by God, you sure are a real pain in the ass!'
He gave the warden another secret wink then quietly,
and oh so innocently, asked, 'Taking medicine, are you, lass?'
Then with his sonsy sunburnt face beaming, mischievously asked,
'Oh, an' why are you taking medicine, hen?...
are you no'weel?'

Suicide Island

Happy fishers on large, lovely, Loch Crocach
unthinking row past a vivid green island,
an island where some suicides and one murderer
are buried; perhaps they lie uneasy in that
unhallowed, unconsecrated ground,
for, if local legend is believed,
eerie nocturnal wailings and other
unnatural banshee sounds are often heard around
this lush, emerald green island.
On this loch's many small islands dense thickets
of birch, rowan, willow and hazel thrive, all safe from
questing teeth of hungry sheep.
Even on bare, gaunt, protruding rocks
tenacious dwarf rowans bravely cling,
cling and urgent clamber skyward
in a desperate struggle to thrive,
or at least stay alive.

Yet on lush green, verdant fertile Suicide Island
not one tree grows; inexplicably, not even one
of these ubiquitous trees, the magic, mystic,
widespread rowan.
Are they prevented perhaps by things
deeper and darker than human logic knows?

Easy to scoff and carefree laugh when passing this island
with fishing friends, all beerily cheery,
everything bright in smiling sunlight;
easy then to dismiss this island's grim history
and ignore its shrouded mystery.
Oh, but its a different story quite
when passing here alone at night!

Rust-Red Wreck

While being fussily towed by small, insolent, sea-going tugs
on what was to be her last voyage –
a journey of ignominy to Rosyth's ship-breaking yard –
that old, still proud, Atlantic liner conspired with a sudden
North Westerly gale to snap all the tugs constraining cables,
then, unmanned, madly raced for land.
Much better to wilful wreck herself
on the jagged rocks of Assynt's savage shore
than to painful slowly and oh so ignominiously
die under the unfeeling mercenary eye
of profit seeking ship-breaker.

The gale seemed to eager ally itself to that liner's
desperate attempt to escape the disgrace of a cruel, inglorious,
ship-breaking fate as, getting fiercer and fiercer,
it cheered her on with collusive strength,
unerring steered her past Loch Dhrombaig's scattered,
spray-battered rocky isles then heaved her impressive length
high ashore on an exposed mainland bay.
And there to this day the remains of that once proud
and massive Atlantic liner lie
and still its vivid rust-reds vie
with the russet-reds of gale flattened winter bracken.

Stoat

Concealed within sleek body's Winter coat that's turned it completely
snowy-white, but for that neat black-tipped tail,
that hungry hunting stoat spreads terrifying fear,
brings swift, merciless death.
Its tenacious vice-like grip holds rabbit's red-gurgling throat;
large hind legs give final feeble kicks,
ebbing life despairing gives up all hope...
Death as certain, as relentless, as hangman's choking rope.

Natural Conservationist
(in memory of Donald MacLeod)

Donald Pollochan, an ageing Achmelivich crofter
contentedly smoked his favourite old pipe as, steadily
and effortlessly, I row us up the narrow, rock-girthed length
of beautiful Loch Roe.
We were on a self-imposed mission of natural conservation...
Conservation not college taught, but direct knowledge
garnered by Pollochan's many years of keen observation
to become that impressive marvel his vast store
of deep, accurate, Nature Lore.

Both shotguns accurate blasts of heavy buckshot
kill three Great Black-Back Gulls;
these huge, powerful, ruthless predators had brought terror
and savage death to this long-established colony
of dainty Arctic Terns.
Landing on the Terns small, rugged, nesting isle
Pollochan and I are delighted to find many eggs
tucked safe and snug in shallow nests.
We are surprised and further delighted as bleak bare rock
sudden comes alive and five fluffy Tern chicks
magically materialize;
then, obeying distraught parents agitated cries,
these chicks again crouch motionless
and again turn to stone.

Leaving these – we hope – now quite safe chicks
and those graceful, though agitated, low-swooping
'Sea-Swallows' in peace, we haste away.
After collecting some seagulls large and – as Pollochan
assured me – quite tasty, already well-salted eggs,
I steadily rowed back down Loch Roe on our homeward way.

We securely moor Pollachan's immaculate sturdy boat;
we walk the path through his neat croft's
verdant hay meadow.
We smile as a Corncrake ungainly deserts this path
for a ditch's concealing lushness.
Pollochan, that Natural Conservationist, does what he can
to conserve these rare – and becoming rarer – dowdy birds;
he does this despite their persistent nocturnal din;
he generously forgives them the insistent monotony
of their rasping, sleep-disturbing, disyllabic sounds.

Hedonists

See these children at last complete their sandcastle;
after all their intense concentrated play at Achmelivich's
wondrous gleaming white sands they ponder which final shell
to place in which way.
After setting brave banners of gulls feathers, black and white and grey,
they, with care and pride, hoist on the highest tower
a Union Jack, all bright red, blue and white.

What that the Minch's rising tide will soon wash all
their fine work away,
they have gloried in all this bright, all-engrossing play.
We, like they, most enjoy our life's all too brief day
before time's relentless tide all too soon washes us away!

A Unique Spirit Level?

See that neat Dipper nonchalant bob underwater,
see him immaculate clad in jacket's formal black
and white bib's stiff starch.
Watch him walk under winking water,
see him stalk round glinting stones
quite at home in this Assynt Burn's
rushing runs and tumbling turns.

Does air trapped in his feathery back
give quicksilver gleams of ethereal delight
and sparkle sequin visions of aquatic dances?
Or is that trapped bubble of air a rather erratic,
a not very accurate spirit level
that gaily takes the measure
of that Dipper's underwater feeding pleasure?

Killer Whales

Contentedly rowing homeward after my pleasant fishing trip
I leisurely enjoy this perfect summer evening's vivid sunset glow.
Entering narrow Loch Roe my startled senses are assaulted
by an ugly bedlam of gulls demented screechings
and I sense a terrible tension all around.

Calm sea is violent torn apart... porpoises lead the way,
not their usual graceful curving play
but, driven by some overwhelming fear,
they arrow high through dusk's alarmed sky.
A shoal of mackerel sudden appear,
also urged by a terrible fear they leap as one
then urgent race for open sea.

In answer to my astounded wonder three Killer Whales
volcanic rise... rise near, far too near, to me!
Well aware of the all too real menace of these
primeval killers I, too, experience deep instinctive fear;
all too conscious of the vulnerability of my small boat
I instantly shed civilizations terribly thin veneer!

As one, these three killer Whales turn...
Turn and come direct for me with steady,
and it seems, deadly intent!
As these killing monsters surge towards me
I urge my boat for rocky shore with urgent oars.

I nervous wait poised ready to leap ashore,
ready to leave my boat to its fate,
but, after surging inquisitively near,
these three Killer Whales turn and gently glide away.
It seems they are not in a hunting, killing mood,
may well be replete with food
having made good meals of porpoises and of seals.

As I row further into Loch Roe I see strange movements
on grey rocks and hear plaintive sounds.
Safely high above highest tide line some seals
are rhythmic swaying their distraught bodies,
are weeping and wailing and, it seems, are unavailing
praying for their savaged companions
or for their murdered pups.

Rowing through a repulsive slick of dispersing blood
I scatter noisy gulls still greedy squabbling
over the last small scraps of torn flesh.
After securing my boat at its moorings I, fish-laden,
hurry homeward eager to no longer hear
these dreadful doleful wailings from these
grief demented seals, but still these terrible laments
eerily haunt me as they follow me and seem to further
grimly dim this dusk-dimmed bay.

Air Mail

These small, downy neat, fast growing Mallard ducklings
vigorously paddle with hidden feet;
they travel their restless trail by surface mail,
then they halt and stretch compact bodies high,
extend straight necks, unhinge and eagerly flap
tiny postage stamp wings.

Oh be patient, many delicious Summer months must pass
before you fly, before you glory through freedom's sky
with wings that soar by air-mail.

Foolish Self-Applause

Silent gliding then skilful twisting between trees
that relentless sparrow-hawk snatched its hapless prey.
There's an explosion of feathers, a screech of frantic fear.
Terrified woodpigeon splatter, clatter, scatter up through trees,
up, up, and away on loud clapping, self-applauding wings.
As they indulge in this drum-beating foolish self-praise
these pigeons think themselves quite brilliant
to have so cleverly evaded that deadly predator.

Foolishly rejoicing, these boastful pigeons rise ever higher
into the clear, bright, summer sky
all blissfully unaware of any danger lurking there.
But this apparently safe wide sky
is where a keen-eyed peregrine-falcon alertly flys
with one already selected pigeon as its unwary prey.
That falcon almost vertical drops in a thrilling, skilful
accurate killing dive and with almost nonchalant ease
snatches a foolish boastful pigeon from the innocent sky.

Loch Roe Poachers

The midnight tide has turned, so now our poaching work is done;
we poach not for love of mercenary money
but more for love of poachings companionable fun,
for its exciting continuation of grand ancestral habits.
Our half dozen fine salmon will be freely shared with
our old, frail, deeply appreciative Achmelvich neighbours.
Quickly, but neatly, we stack away our guiltily wet
illicit net into concealing canvas sack.
As each salmon is gently lifted we nautical burglars
lovingly admire its perfect streamlined shape;
we gloat with something like Pagan pleasure
over the beauteous treasure of its mint-silver glitter.
Then all this piratical swag is hid away
in another cavernous – mouthed canvas sack.

Now, with this treasure of Loch Roe's bounty –
this boat load of booty – pleasantly secure we have
leisure to look around before we wash away these tell-tale
salmon scales that gleam the hull's clinkered larch
and ghost the floorboards a strange phantasmal glow.
As dark gets darker our boat's bright wake gets brighter
and leaves a wide phosphorescent track that glitters
like a flaring comet's flamboyant tail,
that glimmers brighter than full moon's ocean reflected glory,
that is straighter far than slimy snail's drunken trail.

As each oar splashless dips, rhythmic glides, then smooth rises
it gives gentle chuckles and ceaseless drips myriads of
phosphorescent stars that are wondrous miniature galaxies
whose glittery glories almost rival the night sky's
mysterious distant marvels.
The two older of these camaraderie poachers
relax in contented ease while the youngest poacher
willing guides them homeward with skilful tireless oars.
Pollochan's favourite old pipe trails its soothing mellow scent;
MacCaig's cigarette insistent adds its clashing fragrance.
The Achmelvich crofter nostalgically re-tells
a grand ancestral story;
the modest poet secretly dreams of eventually
('when recollecting in tranquillity') making this thrilling
experience poetically live on, perhaps even make this
poaching trip trail Wordsworthian worthy 'clouds of glory'

The Tourists Eagle

With what breathless haste excited tourists gasp out
their wondrous tales of having seen and photo'ed
not just one, but two eagles perched on roadside fence posts.
We used to quietly correct them, sorrowfully inform them
that these impressive birds were not golden eagles,
were merely common-buzzards.
They were so terribly disappointed at having their golden
illusions shattered that eventually we decided it was much
kinder not to reveal the much too cruel truth.

So now, listening with deep interest, keeping a strict
straight face, we hide our doubts, we let excited tourists
retain their golden dreams of having so closely seen
these golden eagles.
We locals have now secretly re-named the common-buzzard,
it is now genially known as 'The Tourists Eagle.'

Little wonder if our common Highland buzzards
now suffer from illusions of grandeur, think themselves
metamorphosed into noble golden eagles as they boastful
soar impressively high and spiral wide with conscious pride
before dropping to perch on lowly fence post or tall pole
and once more resume their deceitful, photogenic role
of 'The Tourists Eagle'.

It's almost as though they proudly know
that they now compete with the Loch Ness Monster
as one of the Highlands most eagerly sought after
tourist attractions...
And don't those 'Tourists Eagles'
put on a much more constant show!

Red Squirrels

Mysterious Dusk

As sunset reluctant fades away dusk's gathering darkness
conquers last of lingering day,
it makes our oars luxuriant drip entire galaxies
of fluorescent stars
while our easy rowing sets the sturdy old boat's wake
all ghostly glowing.

As dusk grows ever darker daytime's familiar scene
transmutes to a place of subtle mystery where the gentle sea
seems to sadly sigh and the shadowy land
becomes an unknown entity where only unseen
nocturnal predatory creatures stealthily pace.

At this time that is neither clear day nor quite
true night, everything seems mysteriously eerie;
normal life seems suspended, must be held in trust
while strange imaginings are given birth.........
see that sinisterly slithery seaweed suggest the
blindly groping fingers of this sea's unburied bloated dead.
Then imagination conjures more pleasant visions....
That ever restless seaweed is now more like some
innocent maiden's dark spreading tresses
which the lonely tide gently strokes and lovingly caresses.

This is a time and place full of strange Primeval mystery;
at times it even gives tantalising hints of wondrous
Mystic Mystery; yes, there is a strange, shadowy, unreal feel
about this time and place, yet this unique strangeness
somehow feels more intensely real than common day's
'normal' reality.
There is a wondrous deep peace; there is true harmony
between men and boat; between boat and sea;
between sea, shadowy land and star-smiling sky.
We quietly contented fishermen are fulfilling our correct role,
are an intrinsic part of Nature;
we and Dusk's whispering sea form a grand unity,
are part of one vast, glorious, harmonious Whole!

A Lazy Wind
(In memory of Dougie Munro)

I hurry homeward across Achmelvich Bay's sand dunes
eager to get out of this fierce, freezing Northerly wind
that playful seeming flutters some snow flakes on its
cruel, knife-edged breath,
that savage flings high white spumes of salty spray,
that keen whistles, lifts and spreads in fresh drifts
these dry white sands that attack my half-closed eyes.

I sudden see another hurrying figure, another man with
hunched shoulders and chest-buried chin,
we quickly meet and I cheerily greet that local crofter,
that fine friend, Dougie Munro.
As we halt and turn our backs against the cruel blast
I gasp, 'That's a real snell wind!'

'Aye,' Dougie feelingly agrees, 'It's a real lazy wind!'
Puzzled, I ask, 'A lazy wind?'
Dougie gave his ready hearty laugh then grinned,
'Aye, it's a wind that's too lazy to go all the way
around a body, but goes icily slicing straight through
shivering human flesh!'
Laughing, we part and continue struggling homeward
through that cruely lazy Northerly wind.

Loyalty Rewarded

Thicker and ever more impenetrably thicker drifts this
November mist; in collusion with a dismal soaking drizzle
it turns this familiar Assynt landscape into a dreich
misery of utter confusion.
With malicious clinging insistence it drenched the
widespread heather and beady dripped from dying
withered bracken.
It slickly smoothed the silky coats of dismally
shivering setters; it soaked the bedraggled shaggy coats
of tough, hard-working fox-terriers.
With cruel persistence this clinging drizzle soaked through
the young trainee gamekeeper's first pair of thick Plus-fours,
it conjured out from these Assynt Estate tweeds
that subtly unique damp tweedy smell which in future
Assynt years he was to get to know so well.

As this insistent mist and drizzle hasten dreich November's
dismal dark the young gamekeeper is thankful to have these dogs,
these ever loyal companions, with him; they seem to have more
confidence in his route finding skills than he has himself
as he sudden comes across a group of stunted birches where
no trees should be, and then, dismayed and confused,
has to turn back from a squelchy black quagmire where he
had expected to find safe firm ground.
Then at last he thankful stumbles on something definite...
That well known track that'll lead him back to Torbreck,
back to the welcome kennels and happy dogs waiting food.

And here at Torbreck that novice gamekeeper and the late
but safe returned dogs receive a warm relieved welcome
from Bod MacDonald, the gamekeeper in charge who with his
experienced years had greatly feared that some mishap had befallen
that inexperienced lad.
As it had got ever later, Bob had got even more worried,
had thought that a search-party might soon be required
to go and find that missing lad, perhaps find him hopelessly lost
or even in some much worse, much more dire trouble.
Bob, and his terribly worried waiting sisters, are profoundly
thankful that there's now no need for any search-party.
Little did these greatly relieved Torbreck gamekeepers guess
just how soon they *would* be out searching in tonight's
dreadful drizzly dark,
for not everyone was as fortunate as that trainee gamekeeper.

Long after this bleak November day's early dark an
amazingly fit eighty year old crofter had still not returned
to his Brackloch croft after being out checking his sheep,
accompanied, as always, by his faithful old collie dog.
The alarm is raised, gamekeepers and neighbouring crofters
set out in search; they plunge through midnight's dismal dark;
some plunge thigh deep in freezing burns, others, cursing,
flounder into quaky bog but none see any sign
of missing old crofter or of his collie dog.
As torch batteries give up the ghost these soaking searchers agree
they've done all that can be done in this miserable darkness;
'Aye,' a soaking and weary old crofter ruefully remarks,
'the nicht's as dark as the inside o' a big black cat!'

Day after miserably drizzly day they, and many others,
unavailing search that not high nor remote, but ruggedly
rough Assynt land North of Brackloch.
They skirt around its large lochs, they search its many
half-hidden lochans, they cautiously inspect its all too many
peat black, sheep-devouring quagmires,
they climb each steep rocky and heathery knoll,
but still none find any trace of lost old crofter
or of his faithful old collie.
Now these searchers voice their secret thoughts:
that poor old crofter's body might never be found,
he might be drowned in some obscure lochan.
Others fear he might have disappeared into some bottomless bog.
Perhaps the old crofter and his old collie dog, inseparable in life
are now inseparably buried together, are swallowed up in death's
peat-black quagmire.
In the final hour of the final day's despairing search
the body of the old Brackloch crofter was found...
Was discovered huddled under an overhanging peat bank
where, weak and emaciated, his faithful old collie
still lay and loyally guarded his loved master's cold corpse.
For all those many long, miserable, days and nights had
saved his master's body from suffering the ugly indignities
that hungry predators scavenging teeth or beaks would
have ruthlessly inflicted.

A young *Sunday Post* reporter had helped in this final search,
now he was rewarded with this fine exclusive scoop.
With photo and admiring story he blazed the glory
of this ever faithful Brackloch collie.
Scotland's quaint, unique, favourite family newspaper fairly
went to town with this heart-warming sentimental story;
it gushing touched many quivering dog-loving hearts
not only all over Scotland, but all over Britain,
and then overseas as that *Sunday Post* reached Scots
exiles in Canada, Australia and New Zealand.

The old Brachloch collie, unaware of his sudden fame,
looks on with disdain at these heaped parcels of gifts, these
generous rewards sends to him from British and overseas dog-lovers
for his devoted loyalty to his dead master.
Cosy in the unaccustomed luxury of his gifted dog-basket
he sleeps and, as thumping tail and eager moving paws prove,
dreams.... Joyous dreams of that old Brackloch crofter
and him being again together, being out in the best, or worst
of weather, of his accurate racing through soaking heather.
It seems that in his sleep that tireless old collie is still
obeying his master's whistled orders, is still up to gathering in
even the most scattered, most unruly Assynt sheep.

With patient tolerance the Brackloch collie allows some
of the least pretentiously expensive gifted collars to be
fastened around his neck, but oh how he hates to try on
some of the many gifted dog-coats; when given laughing permission
oh with what disdainful vigour he shakes off these
silly sissy coats.
He can tolerate being unaccustomed pampered, can be
seduced by exotic gifted food, but he's certainly not
reduced to wearing such fancy nancy coats.
How could he look another crofter's collie in the eye
while wearing such a fancy garment?
These bright waterproof coats are stupid un-necessary follies,
are an insult to him and to the entire race of crofters
and shepherds hardy, loyal, hard-working Collies!

A Sure Midge Repellent

The young trainee ghillie revelled in the great privilege
of fishing for salmon in this salmon-rich River Inver;
only one thing prevented this bliss from being perfect –
those dementing swarms of stinging midges!
As the tormented ghillie clawed his midge assaulted head
Charlie Ross, that grand, experienced, Assynt gamekeeper said,
'Do you want to ken an efficient midge repellent?....
A sure way tae keep thae hellish midges at bay.'
'Aye, I certainly do!.... Is there such a thing?' eagerly,
perhaps rather naively, the novice ghillie asks with disbelief,
with his face a mass of maddening midge stings.
'Aye,' he was solemnly assured, 'all you have tae dae
when it's awful midgy is tae get a bottle o' whisky
and pour a grand dram ower the top o' your head.'

'Are you sure?... Is that a certain midge cure?'....
The young gillie thought it most unlikely,
surely those awful blood-thirsty Assynt midges
would relish the whisky, would delight in getting tight!
'Is this true? Have you tried that whisky repellent?....
Does it work for you?'

'Oh aye, I've tried it, 'Charlie said. Then, with
ruddy face beaming, with eyes gleaming with mischievous
mirth explained...
'Aye, I've unsuccessfully tried it, but I find the trouble
with that repellent is that somehow I can never
get the whisky up tae the top o' ma head,
somehow the whisky bottle aye goes tae ma mooth instead!'

Almost Disgraced

Today there is to be no strenuous game-keeping work for me
on Assynt's deer grazed hills, its grouse moors nor at its
attractive trout lochs or salmon-filled rivers;
instead I was requested to help an elderly Lady,
a wealthy, titled, English aristocrat, an expert entomologist,
to find a very special rare moth that's only found
where sea and heather meet.

Soon that Lady and I are diligently searching the
shoreline heather near Lochinver's almost tide-girth Kirk.
As I carry a large butterfly net at the ready I furtive
glance around and fervent pray that none of my hardy
climbing pals from Glasgow, now camping at Achmelvich Bay,
will appear and see me employed in this sissy way.

All too vividly I imagine their cutting remarks, their rude
jokes and jeers. With them in past years I had tackled
The Cobbler's hardest rock routes, had faced the challenge
of Ben Nevis's exhilarating winter gullies;
had even - thankfully rarely - scarily precariously
climbed with a slightly less mad members of the famous -
or infamous? - Greagh Dhu climbing club.
Had watched with awe as I saw one of the most fabulously
erratic of that club's wildly crazy climbers tackle
a very severe new rock route, his endangered head
impressively protected by an ex-German Army steel bucket helmet.
I discovered later the secret of that German helmet's
other use as, accompanied by resounding laughter,
it passed around as a commodious chamber-pot
when Glencoe's snugly crowded Jacksonville Bothy
was ferociously storm bound.

Now, after such exciting adventures, am I reduced to this...
to fluttering about with a butterfly net?
How will I ever live down the disgrace if these hardy
climbing pals should see me now?
How will I ever look them in the face?

As I continued my diligent search I cannot help thinking
that this is quite some come-down from risking life and limb
on Summer's precarious mountain rock and on Winter's
sometimes decidedly dicey ice.
Then I spy, eagerly chase after, and finally capture
not just one, but two of those rare moths.
The delighted Lady, in clear, distinctive, toff voice
loudly exclaims, 'Oh, jolly good show!...
Oh, how clever of you, Robert!'
Again I cast a quick furtive glance,
again am delighted that none of my hardy Glasgow pals
are near to hear!

As, pleased with the success of our hardly intrepid hunting,
we drive away in the Lady's posh Rolls-Royce and return up
the narrow private road to Glen Canisp Shooting Lodge
we sudden meet some of my climbing pals sweatily returning
from having been climbing that fantastic mountain Suilven.
Impressed by seeing me so stately ensconced in that
Rolls-Royce these Glasgow lads obstreperous laugh and cheer then
with mock obsequiousness bow low, while I, as though
taking their mocking homage seriously, sedately-almost
Queen Motherly - condescendingly wave in return and try
to look as if I, too, have had a sweatily strenuous
day stalking after Assynt's wary red deer stags
instead of sissy searching for silly moths.

A Unique Barometer

After enduring many exhausting, rain and gale battered
stalking hours, after covering many familiar, wildly rugged
Assynt miles, having skinned two accurately shot stags
and left them hanging in the shooting-lodge's deer larder
this day's long stalk on Glen Canisp Deer Forest was,
at last, complete.
Now the two gamekeepers and two ghillies – all weary,
dishevelled, soakingly bedraggled – urgent seek
the sanctuary of the lodge's gun-room.

Once the rifle has been quickly, expertly, dried, cleaned, oiled,
then securely locked away the younger gamekeeper ventures
into the kitchen, tries not to sully this, the housekeeper's
spotless domain while the others remain in the gun-room
and pray that she will be in a good mood today.

Their eyes bright gleam their ruddy faces beam
as the young 'keeper returns with a well-laden, glass-tinkling tray.
The head-gamekeeper's expert gaze lasers onto the
four glasses, his experienced eyes accurately measure each dram,
he gives a resounding laugh then voices all their thoughts:
'Oh, thank God, the housekeeper's again been generous
with oor drams; obviously we're back in her good books!'
With glass held high he again laughs:
'Long may her good mood last!'
With heartfelt cries of 'Slainte!' four glasses clink together,
four generous drams fly to four parched mooths,
are gulped down with well-practised skill and four
terrible Highland drouths get delightful relief.
Such drams are undoubtedly the greatest, the best loved,

traditional perquisites that these Highland stalkers
receive at the end of each long, wet, tiring, deer-stalking day.
The amount of whisky in each glass was an accurate
barometer which measured the mood of this shooting-lodge's
housekeeper;
when her outlook was bright and sunny the whisky rose
high in the glasses, but when her mood was stormy or dour
the level of whisky decidedly crept measurably, dejectedly lower!

The head-gamekeeper grinned around at the surrounding men,
all these ruddy, weather-beaten faces glowed and beamed
ever redder, all well stoked with grand whisky's genial fire;
all nodded their furnace heads in sage agreement as he said:
'We must all dae oor utmost tae keep in favour
with the housekeeper; must dae nothing tae upset her,
dae nothing tae make her barometer drop once mair.
We must try tae ensure that oor drams
continue tae reach damn near the top o' oor glasses.....
Ensure that her unique whisky barometer remains steady set at "Fair"!'

True Elements
(1)

Watch those two mated swans plod down that pebble beach,
how labourious, how ungainly, how undignified
is that footsore waddling walk.
But oh what a difference when they reach
the calm fresh waters healthy welcome embrace...
do they sigh with relief?
Do they complain of their poor aching feet?
Do they know how this, their true element,
instant transmutes them to things of utmost grace,
things of pure, glittering, perfect beauty?

True Elements
(2)

When young I had thankfully fled the city's grim ways,
had escape the choking traffic's soul-destroying roar,
had wisely spent my best years climbing Highland hills.
Had then wondrous fished high remote secret Assynt lochs
with her I loved.
Together in our true element we lived, loved and fished
for many well contented years
under our wide, windswept, happy Assynt sky.

Chief's Burial Isle

That small, stark, rocky isle anchored in Loch Assynt's
remote Tubeg Bay contains the decaying bones of buried Chiefs,
the mouldering remains of once proud MacLeod warriors,
the fierce, feared, undisputed leaders of their Assynt Clan.
Now they lie close packed in that small isle's shallow graves,
unseemly stacked, plaid wrapped, man on man.

Once haughty bones now mingle in layers of common dust,
yellow teeth devilish grin, dark eye-sockets blankly gape,
ancient rib cages collapse and promiscuous intermingle
with once keen claymores that now slowly decay to rust.

In turn each Chief's body was slowly mournfully carried
from Ardvreck Castle that stronghold of their pride,
their vain pomp and great power
which time and weather will in due course together
reduce to one sorry, neglected, crumbling tower.
Conveyed by his mourning Clansmen, convoyed by his
personal piper's dismal wailing lament
each Chief crossed Loch Assynt on his final journey.
Each fleet of small boats bravely defied the loch's
wild windswept miles,
untiring rowed their fallen Chief to that remote bay's
darkly grey cairned isle.
Each Chief died surrounded by genuine grief,
died happy in knowledge that he would quietly rest
buried with his Clan's best;
would lie there untroubled, knowing that no uneasy soul
can travel over this stretch of fresh water;
knowing that his mouldering remains would forever remain
secure and undisturbed on this ancestral Burial Isle.
In truth Loch Assynt's protective expanse of fresh water

did prove true to those ancient Highland legends,
did save each Assynt Chief's menaced soul...
or at least saved every Chief's shallow buried body,
protected them not from ghostly prowling ghosts and ghouls
but from much more real menace of fierce-prowling,
keen-digging, hunger-drooling wolves.

Penicillin Pete
(A Story)

Norman Peter MacInnes was an eighty four year old crofter. He was a bachelor. His un-married sister, Janet, had kept house for him, had insisted he shaved at least once per week and that he accompanied her to Kirk each Sabbath. Since her death a few years ago he no longer shaved and no longer went to Kirk. He felt all the better for these two neglects.

Local crofters affectionately thought of him as a 'character'; one of the few, once numerous, real 'auld worthies' still alive in Assynt.

Norman revelled in playing up to his role as a 'character'; he still greatly enjoyed a good dram and a good laugh. He refused to waste the few remaining years of his long life on such drearily boring things as housework or too much washing of his clothes or even of himself.

Norman – or 'Norman Peter', as he was known locally – happily shared his neglected untidy crofthouse with one companion, his auld collie, Rab. The crofter and the dog suffered from failing eyesight. When Norman tripped over Rab, or the sleeping collie was stood on, the old man and old dog snarled and swore at one another for a quite enjoyable lively few moments.

One particularly dreich and miserable November day auld Rab was lying contentedly stretched out warming his old bones in front of the kitchen fire. He was sound asleep. In the dimness of the late afternoon gloom his master stumbled and stood on one of Rab's outstretched legs.

The old collie instantly sprang from deep sleep to self-defence. He instinctively snapped at Norman's ankle.

The startled old crofter vividly cursed as he staggered to a chair.

Ashamed of his inexcusable deed, Rab apologetically sidled over to beloved master and begged to be forgiven. He was.

As 'Norman Peter' examined his wounded ankle there was a knock at the door, it opened and Doctor Fraser stepped in.

'Och, it's yourself, doctor. Come away in,' Norman hospitably called as he tried to hide his injured ankle behind his other ankle.

The doctor observed his action, 'It something wrong with your foot, Norman?'

Doctor Fraser was the local general practitioner. Based at Lochinver village, his practise covered all of the vast, wildly ragged district of Assynt. Often, when calling on other crofter patients living near Norman, he made a point of looking in to see how the solitary old man was keeping.

The doctor was well aware of how reluctant the thrawn auld bugger was to request his assistance. He greatly admired the toughness and self-reliant independent spirit of 'Norman Peter.' He wished that some of his much younger patients, all too frequent callers at his surgery, had half the toughness and resolute strength of that old crofter.

'What's wrong with your foot?' Doctor Fraser again asked.

'Och, it's nothing much, doctor. It's just a wee bit scratch at ma ankle.' He explained what had happened.

'You'd better let me have a look at it. Any dog bite is potentially dangerous.'

'Och, it's nae worth bothering wi', doctor.'

The doctor insisted. Norman reluctantly revealed his injured foot. 'Take your sock off,' Doctor Fraser ordered.

'Ma sock is off, doctor.'

Startled out of his professional calm, the doctor exclaimed, 'Good Lord, I thought that was a dark sock on your foot!' Peering more closely through the dimness he saw that the foot was shadowed with dirt. Recovering himself, he said, 'I'm sorry. It's so dim in here I can't see properly. I'll switch on the electric light.'

'Aye, go ahead, doctor. Och but this new-fangled eelectricity is real braw, isn't it? I find it real fine an'dandy tae switch on the eelectric tae see tae trim an' light ma' paraffin lamps!'

'You're joking, aren't you, Norman?'

'Norman Peter' beamed and laughed, 'Aye, chust ma' wee joke, doctor.'

As Doctor Fraser went to the doorway and switched on the 'eelectric' light he had a startling thought: 'I wonder how many baths old Norman's had since his sister's death?'

While he cleaned away the dirt and blood from the wounded ankle the doctor secretly smiled to himself as he answered his own question, 'Damned few, if any!'

And yet, despite the unwashed state of the hardy old man's body and clothes, he remained much fitter than many a carbolicly clean man half his age. *Despite* his unwashed state? The doctor wondered, again smiling to himself. He knew that 'Norman Peter' and quite a few other of his oldest, fiercely independent minded patients assured him that they kept their amazingly robust health and fitness *because* of unwashed state. They argued that too many baths or showers just washed away the body's natural defences. As a young, up-to-date physician, Doctor Fraser could not agree with this theory - it was ridiculous! (Many years later he was to thoughtfully remember this stoutly asserted belief of those old people when he read a persuasive article in a medical journal written by an eminent microbiologist. This scientist agreed with them: too many hot baths or showers *did* reduce the body's natural defences by reducing the amount of necessary bacteria on the human skin.)

'That's the bite cleaned, Norman. It's not deep, it's not bleeding now.'

'Och, doctor, I told you it was only a scratch. I'm sorry tae gie you a' this trouble.'

'It's no trouble,' Doctor Fraser replied as he spread antibiotic powder over the injury then covered it with a large plaster.

Rab, the contrite old collie, anxiously looked on as the doctor attended to his injured and generously forgiving master. Doctor Fraser again hid a smile as he said, 'You can put your sock back on now, Norman. I'll go to my car and get a syringe for an anti-tetanus injection.'

As he turned, the doctor patted Rab and grinned, 'Oh, you old rascal, what do you mean by biting your master?'

Norman was delighted to see the doctor in such a pleasant mood, 'Och, he couldn't help it. He didn't mean onie harm. It's gey good o' you tae gie him a tetanus jab.'

The doctor stared in astonishment, 'What are you talking about, Norman? The anti-tetinus injection is for you.'

'Och, doctor, I don't need onie injection. Go on, gie it tae Auld Rab.'

Doctor Fraser opened his mouth to argue, then, thinking of the filthy state of Norman's foot, he lost his customary professional dignity; he burst into laughter. 'By God, Norman,' he gasped, 'Aye, right enough the poor dog is probably in much greater need of the anti-tetanus injection than you - you tough old bugger - are!'

Old Norman heartily joined in the doctor's laughter then said, 'Instead o' onie injection I'll tak' the best medicine - a dram - a damn big dram! You'll tak' a dram wi' me, won't you, doctor?'

Doctor Fraser started to refuse: he never drank while on duty. But he smiled and relented. He would break his own strict rule this once. 'Thanks, Norman, but make it a very wee dram.'

Norman thrust a full whisky bottle and an empty glass at him. 'Here, doctor, help yourself. Tak' as much or as little as you want.'

'Thank you, Norman.' Furtively he examined the glass. It was none too clean. 'Oh well,' he thought, 'what the hell! Hopefully the strong neat whisky will kill all germs in this glass.'

They both gave the traditional Highland toast of 'Slainte Mhath!'

Once the whisky burned its way down the doctor's throat he gasped and grimaced. His eyes watered. 'By God,' he thought, 'that certainly should kill all known germs!' He managed a smile, 'Did you make this "firewater" yourself, Norman?'

'Och no, doctor. It's a gey puckle o' years since I had ma' ain whisky still.' After taking another big gulp of whisky old 'Norman Peter' sighed contentedly. He was not in the least discomposed by its raw strength. He now hospitably urged, 'Drink up, doctor, drink up. And sit doon; sit doon and mak' yourself at hame.'

They sat down at the kitchen table and old Norman comfortably rested an elbow on it. Doctor Fraser inspected the littered table then gently eased his chair away from it.

'Whit's the matter, doctor? Mak' yourself comfortable there.'

'I'm fine, Norman, I'm fine.'

While the old crofter was engrossed in lovingly gulping more whisky the doctor scrutinised the untidy table. It was a truly amazing mess. Probably it had not been really cleaned since the death of Norman's sister. The oilcloth table cover had originally been chequered with neat red and white squares, but these squares were now difficult to make out under a widespread mass of fungi-like growths. There were lively moulds of varied colours - sickly greens, pale blues, revolting yellows and un-regal purples. Some moulds luxuriously spouted what looked like an old man's three week stubble of white beard. A brown china teapot, jars of jams and marmalade, sauce and pickle bottles, were all neatly fitted into their own sacrosanct places and rose like mini-mountains from this table's weird science fiction landscape.

As Doctor Fraser eased his chair further away from this fantastic table he suggested, 'Oh, Norman, don't you think it's about time you got a new table cover, or gave this one a really good scrubbing?'

The old crofter stared at the doctor in genuine surprise, 'Why... Whit's the matter wi' it, man?'

'Oh, Norman, its a disgrace! It's absolutely filthy!'

Old 'Norman Peter' glanced at the familiar table then fixed the doctor with a baleful stare, 'Och, man, I'm fair surprised at you. Surely as a doctor, a man o' science, you should ken that thae fungi growths are gey good for you.' He grinned broadly and proudly, 'Och, doctor, don't you ken that I discovered penicillin long before yon Doctor Fleming did?'

Doctor Fraser again burst into unrestrained laughter. Eventually he managed to gasp, 'Oh, Norman... Norman, you're incorrigible, you're absolutely incorrigible!'

As he drove back to Lochinver the doctor thoughtfully recollected that penicillin had been derived from a green fungi accidentally growing on a neglected mould. He continued his journey in a pleasantly amused, but an increasingly thoughtful mood.

★ ★ ★

It was after this incident that Norman Peter MacInnes acquired his new nickname of 'Penicillin Pete'. He suffered no ill effects from being bitten by his old collie. And, perhaps even more surprisingly, tough Auld Rab was none the worse for having taken a bite at his master's grubby ankle!

Old Dirky

At local crofters urgent request two gamekeepers search
Stoer Point's high, sea-lashed cliffs for foxes secret dens;
one, or more, of these plundering brutes have
savagely killed many young lambs.
Charlie Ross, the head-gamekeeper, releases Dirky, his old,
tough, experienced, fox-hating rough-coated terrier.
Two other terriers keenly follow Old Dirky as he un-erring
leads the way through a jumbled mass of huge boulders
that have tumbled down these steep, dangerous cliffs.

The gamekeeper's patient wait with ready guns outside a
bouldered cave that's littered with mutilated remains
of foxes prey and has that strong musky stink
that only mature male foxes gave.
Suddenly, although expected, still an adrenalin surging shock
as that large male fox urgent bolts...
Two accurate shotgun blasts end that plundering rogue's
desperate dash.
After some time two terriers come up, but despite Charlie's
anxious shouts, there's no sign of Old Dirky.
Hearing his faint answering barks from deep down
in that dark cave, the 'keepers fear that the over-eager
old terrier's got himself hopelessly trapped.
For long tense hours they anxious wait, ever more despairing
continue shouting, then at last have to leave that
poor trapped old dog.
They return the next day, and the next, and the next;
they hope that Old Dirky can reach some of their blindly
thrown food, but they fear his barks, seeming coming from somewhere
deeper
are getting decidedly weaker.
Finally they try a last desperate measure that might kill outright

or might bravely save.
The local Council road-foreman, an expert at blasting Achmelvich,
Stoer and Drumbeg's narrow roads rock-impeded
blind corners, careful places a stick of dynamite
to blow apart a passage-blocking boulder.
The anxious waiting men, deafened by a blizzard
of protesting gulls, hope that blast has not collapsed
the entire cave, has not entombed the dog they hoped to save.

They find the boulder shattered, the cave largely intact.
Dirk's faint barks answer back as Charlie shouts
and valiantly tries to struggle through that dark,
blast-widened gap.
But, with advancing age he's getting too wide of girth;
he's too fond of his wife's excellent home cooking,
is perhaps a bit too fond of happy convivial drams...
Or does his substantial figure reflect his contented
good nature, his honest, ever-ready mirth?

His companion, much younger, much slimmer, ties on the rope,
struggles into the narrow gap.
Impending rocky fingers tear his shirt and claw his back
as he crawls through then gropes deeper and deeper,
cautious advances into the increasing darkness
guided by torch beam's erratic dance.
Then Old Dirky's beam reflecting eyes bright gleam
and man and dog eager meet with joyous greetings.
Carrying the semi-starved, but still tough and heavy enough
old terrier, the young gamekeeper had a rough, sweaty,
steep struggle up from ledge to narrow ledge before he
let Old Dirky free to crawl through that final rocky gap
and be re-united with his delighted master.
Charlie caresses Dirky's grizzled, battle-scarred head,
inspects his ragged, fox-torn ear while ecstatic licking tongue,

joy–squirming body and frantic stubby tail all rejoice.
The old terrier has lost some weight, has bare patches
where rock has scraped, but still seems fit enough.
Charlie laughs, 'Och, Dirky, I doot you would win nae
prize at Crufts!'

Eyes now re–adjusted to bright June light, Old Dirky,
eager as always, leads the way up from what had almost
been his entombing grave.
Luxuriating in being free, he races up a verdant grassy knoll,
stands still, stands tall, head thrown back gives strange wild call,
part bark, part growl, part howl!
Perhaps a challenge to foxes?... to his mortal foes,
those enemies he loved to hate?
Perhaps that uncanny call was to gloatingly say:
'Foxes, you thought Old Dirky, entombed, had met his fate,
but you just wait, soon you'll know I've survived...
Tough Old Dirky has lived to fight another day!'

Dirge

Taking the familiar rough old track I walk back
through Glen Canisp, and passing ruined Suileag
I once again note how its iron roof –
all bright rust red – weary droops,
loosely hangs and loudly clangs.
Again I listen to its flapping rusty ridge
as it drums its mournful, gale-conducted dirge.

Are these dreary sounds a lament for the dead?
Are they mourning past inhabitants now mouldering underground?
Is that ruined old house bemoaning its neglected, uninhabited state?
Is it unavailing bewailing its dismal fate?

Politician's Charm
(In memory of a certain Member of Parliament)

By the River Inver the ghillie stands and alertly waits
while 'his gentleman' keenly fishes.
Two elderly ladies, quaint dressed in old-fashioned clothes, appear,
speaking oh so genteelly, these old dears express some wishes.

They desire to know about this salmon fishing;
the ghillie tells of the salmons fantastic life;
gently they ask; 'Isn't killing salmon rather cruel?'
The ghillie emphatic states that all Nature is full of cruel strife.

Now these ladies enquire about the fisherman...
Are informed he is a Member of Parliament, a knight no less!
Impressed, they chatter: 'Is it him? Yes, it looks like him,'
their own well known local M.P.
'Yes, it is he, dear Sir Fred,' they correctly guess.

The fisherman approaches and effortless switches on
his politician's smiling public face.
They are his own constituents, members of his own party.
He overwhelms them with his constant charm;
they are all smiles, all simpering grace.

He assures them that salmon when caught feel very little pain.
His well-practised voice can charm birds from trees;
he persuades them that salmon rather enjoy this fishing game!
His endless charm and genial smiles turn their giddy heads,
they think how, back home, they will impress their friends
with this tale of having met charming dear Sir Fred.

Ever smiling, he waves these greatly impressed ladies out of sight,
then turns and reverts to his normal face.
Annoyed at having lost precious fishing time
he grabs his rod and hurries to the next fishing place.

How he now abuses that pair of dear innocent ladies;
with mocking laughter calls them old and silly;
no need now for politician's deceptive smiling face
and weary sham of constant charm
for his audience is now only his little-regarded Highland Ghillie!

A Perfect Day

Gasping with strenuous effort, buoyed by high hopes, we –
Eileen and me – crest that final steep heathery slope.
We eager greet that unique loch, that sparkling gem
set snug in its Green Corrie that's
tucked away in one of Assynt's remoter places.
Our gleaming eyes greedy drink in this entrancing scene
while happiness – and sweat – glitter our flushed faces.

Large, plump, golden trout rise and suck down that feast
of mayflies that hatch in countless numbers.
Swooping like large, salty, sea-swallows, blackheaded gulls
incessant feed with insatiable greed
on those defenceless flotillas of mayflies.

Our expert cast, feathery delicate tiny dry-flies deceive
some of the most greedy of these feeding trout.
After noon we unashamedly gloat and un-modestly boast
over our wondrous plump trout that, neatly set out,
are a golden dream far more precious
than bullion's arid mercenary gleam.

Later, naked, we swim, we glittery splash, we joyous dash,
uninhibited Pagans, we carefree shout and laugh.
Now our souls and bodies fuse as one.
How June's benevolent sun smiles down
from Assynt's wise, approving sky
while that fantastic mountain, Suilven,
like a robust old Pagan voyeur peeks over a nearby ridge
and surely whole-heartedly approves as we sensuous intertwine
in Love's passionately joyous play
and let our great Love gloriously consummate this Perfect Day.

The Duke's Stone

His Grace the Duke of Sutherland, returning from salmon fishing
at His River Kirkaig, orders His coachman to stop the coach
at the top of Culag Brae;
from there His Grace will walk back to his imposing shooting-lodge
which so grandly dominates Lochinver Bay.
On his own, His Grace strides down the steep rough road,
he stops, he sits on a large flat stone.
This is one of his favourite viewpoints in Assynt;
when His Grace honours this place with His Noble Presence
none but he dare sit on this sacrosanct seat
now locally known as 'The Duke's Stone.'

Comfortably ensconced on His stone it is, in effect, His Throne,
for on this high and mighty seat he is undisputed 'Monarch of
All He Surveys', for whichever way he looks he owns all he sees,
all... all, he owns it all!
He owns all of Assynt, owns almost all of the vast county
of Sutherland that stretches from here by the wild Minch
to the distant grey North Sea.
As He eagerly stares His chest swells with pompous pride,
he is deeply moved... is moved not with aesthetic delight
but with joy at this solid evidence of His landowning power,
His vast influence, His awesome financial might.

Decades pass, that level turf where His Grace's coach turned
and waited at the Kirkaig Estuary is mostly gone,
eroded away by winter waves storming into Inverkirkaig Bay.
The First World War, that mad, sad, mess of mud, blood and gore
came and left many – far too many – names engraved
on Lochinver's granite War Memorial.
The Second World War come and cruelly engraved a few more.
Peace brought a certain crofter back to Assynt,
back to his ancestral Inverkirk home.
Peace brought a certain poet to Assynt,
here he discovered his true spiritual home.
Both these men have a wise, deep love of whisky and of fishing,
it is fated that they should meet, should, over many convivial drams,
over many rather fishy tales, become great friends.

Each passing year strengthens the friendship of these two men.
Angus MacLeod, the crofter, is an experienced poacher,
Norman MacCaig, the poet, is an experienced schoolteacher;
when it comes to poaching and country lore, Angus knows more...
The crofter lightly wears the mantle of teacher
while the poet willingly becomes the assiduous scholar.

Often fortified by many drams, they reluctantly drag themselves
away from gregarious friends and ease out of the bar at the
Culag Hotel – that imposing sandstone edifice that had once
been His Grace's shooting-lodge – and start to carefree walk
the meandering miles to their welcoming homes,
to their waiting – and welcoming? – wives at Inverkirkaig.

Their soaring spirits uproariously greet Suilven,
but as usual that uniquely steep isolated mountain
stonily ignores them as they happily trail by Loch Culag's
sheltered shore. Near the top of Culag Brae
they comfortably ensconce themselves on 'The Duke's Stone',
this no longer sacrosanct ducal throne.

Sitting at contented ease they are laughingly pleased
at the light-hearted way they so keenly and so wisely
discuss, dissect, and oh so neatly, solve any – or all –
of the world's many seeming insoluble problems.
Oh why, they wonder, can't Politicians, Philosophers and Theologians
solve all Mankind's complex problems as leisurely easily as they –
with the assistance of 'bold, inspiring' whisky – can?

With a cigarette in one hand, a half bottle in the other,
each man contentedly sighs;
as each lifts his inspiring whisky his gaze rises to
lingering dusks brilliant sky.
They are silenced by the profoundly solemn wonder of Beauty
as Assynt's noble hills pulse, glow and blush with
the thrill of this vivid sunset's Turnerish glory.

Angus and Norman silent wait while Beauty constellates;
they squirrel emotions – emotions which the poet will later,
'recollecting in tranquillity', transmute to glowing poems...
Inspiring poems in vivid metaphoric praise of this unique
Assynt land... this land these two men uniquely deeply love
and which only they, and such as they,
can really know and truly 'own'.

Miracle

Sweating under the weight of their rucksacks, waterproofs
and all their needful fishing gear
Angus and Norman complain that this Kirkaig path
is getting longer and steeper with each passing year.

At Fion Loch Norman thankfully carelessly throws off his rucksack,
Angus gazed amazed as their full whisky bottle tumbled out,
aghast, he waited to see it smashed.

But when, with malevolent aim, it hit a lurking stone
that stone split
while the whisky bottle rolled then miraculously lay intact!

In stunned amazement neither man knew quite how to react.
Then, hands clasped in mock prayer, Angus says,
'I now believe there is a God, but not your usual Christian God,
but an older Pagan God with even more mysterious ways.

He looks across the loch to towering Suilven,
imagines old Bacchus grinning down from there,
lifts the miraculous bottle, gulps a generous dram...
He's no patience with any silly, genteel, sissy sips!
Shocked nerves now whiskily steadied
Angus and Norman contentedly continue this memorable fishing trip.

The Butler

After dinner that autumn evening the butler, his day's work done,
visits the ghillie's bothy where, at last, he can relax.
The grinning ghillie is amused at the great contrast...
all day that butler had been a perfect servant,
had behaved impeccably, had been dignified politeness personified,
but now in evenings easeful calm he becomes more natural.

The smiling butler produces his well-earned 'perks'...
The best malt whisky and large deluxe Havana cigars;
having learned from 'his betters'
he truly knows how to enjoy the finer things in life.
Soon butler and ghillie are subtly enveloped in whisky's warming glow
and they revel in the gentle calm of cigar's soothing balm.

The ghillie laughs at the butler's amusing tales,
hears animated stories of servants gossip, of petty intrigues,
of the deep feud simmering between butler and housekeeper...
Who is to be top servant, the real boss
in this Glen Canisp Shooting-Lodge?
Soon mellow malt whisky, working its subtle alchemy,
magically shrinks these worries to a less important scale.

The butler now tells of lords and ladies, the upper classes;
his wealthy employers are polo-playing friends of Royalty,
he had been most impressed by top Royalty's
unassuming off-duty manners when, after polo's final chukka,
he had served them tea - a most welcome cuppa -
or, if preferred, brimming glasses of Pimms.

The evening wore on and the ghillie increasingly saw that butler
as one of the last of an endangered species –
the faithful old family retainer – he felt like a biologist
observing possibly the last living Dodo.
Shouldn't there be a society for the preservation of such butlers?
Listening to ever more tales of title wealth
the ghillie, thanks no doubt to whisky's mellow stealth,
was swept back one hundred years.

Was now in Dickensian times, that era when the British Empire
was at the peak of its glorious power, when Life was great
for those few who possessed immense Imperial Wealth,
while for most of the toiling masses there was no real Life;
they briefly existed in miserable squalor, all too quickly died,
and many were only semi–buried in overcrowded cemetery's
overflowing liquid filth.

The ghillie shuddered and returned to the present;
that terrible, that great, Victorian era seemed long since gone,
but here with wealthy Landed Gentry, butlers, housekeepers,
(yes, and ghillies!) it seemed to tenaciously linger on.

In a burlesque display of his best professional manner
the butler obsequiously asks, 'A little more whisky, sir?'
The ghillie keenly joins in this game, 'Oh no, my man,
not a little more... pour me a damn big dram!'
As the butler obediently pours a generous dram the beaming ghillie
reflects on how easy it is to be seduced by wealths privileges.

The whisky-mellow butler vehemently declares that these
upper classes are still needed; needed to lead in war,
needed to develop vast international enterprises;
having well learned evolutions sure lessons
they rapid adapt to ever changing circumstances,
they are not so easily superseded!

To the ghillie, no doubt due to his working-class Glasgow roots,
all these upper-class privileges seem rather unfair,
but then he remembers the history of the Red Clydesiders,
those passionately sincere true Socialists who all swear
to fly the chain-freed triumphant workers Red Flag
above Glasgow's City Chambers at George square.
But where are any of these surviving Red Clydesiders now?
Good Lord, it appears they're mostly with Lord Shinwell
stoutly defending the privileges of Our noble Peers!
Oh no doubt in future years ever more of these 'Champagne Socialists',
these 'Bollinger Bolsheviks' will gain ever more bureaucratic control,
will half-heartedly set the faltering social order
on a watered-down Socialist tack.
Taking another sip of his delicious mellow - and getting mellower -
whisky, enjoying another almost Churchillian soothing Havana cigar
the sublimely relaxed, contentedly at ease smiling ghillie
complacently thought, 'In the meanwhile, "I'm all right, Jack"!'

Almost An Eagle's Meal

Mellow May sunshine glows our upturned faces,
a small steep cliff shelters us from the
surprising coolness of the Eastern breeze.
Eileen's small white poodle, Chico, carefree joyful plays
some yards from where we sit and smile at his
foolish puppyish antics.
As he gives lamb-like vertical leaps
with all four paws in the air at once,
Eileen merrily shouts, 'Oh, Chico, you're such a crazy dunce!'
Lass, my older fox-terrier as usual sits quietly sedate
while her anxious pleading eyes seem to begrudge us
every morsel of food we hungrily ate.

We do not know that other, keener, eyes than ours
were watching that 'lamb' at play,
had already marked it down as easy prey.
There's a sudden air-rending swoosh above our heads
as an eagle dives with half-closed wings,
with yellow talons reaching to grab with deadly grip.
With terrified squeals Chico dashes to be protected
while Lass, true to her fearless terrier breed,
barks and snarls a fierce challenge as she leaps
at that astonished, bewildered, sudden terrified eagle.

The eagle falters and almost stalls as it violent applies
feathery brakes, then frantic wings assault the air
and thankful grab that cool Easterly breeze.
Again majestic, it effortless spirals ever higher
and angry gazes at these alarming creatures
that had so unexpectedly, so dramatically, spoilt her easy kill.
Resuming her hunting she is again keenly conscious of that
hungry chick that's entirely dependent on her predatory skills.

Later, back home, safe within the garden gate,
Chico lies drowsily nearly asleep on fresh mown back lawn,
but when low-flying gulls cast sudden shadows
over him he leaps up with frightened squeals
all too vividly remembering that fearsome time
when he almost became an eagle's meal!

A Dream Realised
(A Story)

The three humans and two dogs in that calmly advancing boat were all quietly happy.

Glen, the black labrador gun–dog and Rab, the fox–hating working terrier, were keenly excited to be going on another expedition with their master. They perched companionably together in the bow and, like restless figure-heads, gazed expectantly ahead.

Their master, Ewan Grant, a not quite twenty six year old gamekeeper, was young enough to also get excited by these various working expeditions. Today his controlled excitement and quiet happiness were made all the greater by him having his fiancée, Lorna MacLeod, sitting beside him in the centre of this boat and by him holding and affectionately squeezing her warmly responsive hand.

But perhaps even happier than any of the others in this crowded boat was Duncan Stewart. As he sat in the stern, his right hand guiding the powerful outboard motor, his eyes bright with deeply pleasurable contentment, he felt something like platonic love for those two happily self-engrossed lovers sitting on that seat in front of him, their backs to him.

Duncan's quietly ecstatic gaze thirstily drank in the widespread beauty of this passing West Highland scene. As this long freshwater loch narrowed, the steep, tree-less heather hills on both sides sloped even steeper and urgent hurried down to meet the thickly brackened shores.

How wonderful, how almost unbelievably wonderful, that this trout-rich loch and these deer-rich hills were now his long dreampt of, his finally realised, work-place!

How gloriously different from what until a few months ago had been his working background. As a Glasgow postman his work-place had been that sprawling city's endless grey streets, its renovated tenements and its ugly, overcrowded high-rise flats.

Whenever his work allowed Duncan had got out of Glasgow. As an excited eager youth he'd almost worshipingly followed in the footsteps of old

Tom Weir as he blazed his inspiring mountain trail all over his beloved Scottish hills.

Then as a young man, Duncan had discovered the wild glory of the North West Scottish Highlands.

He had met and become a great friend of the only slightly older Ewan Grant. In the last few years Duncan had spent his summer holidays working with Ewan and his wealthy boss as a part-time fishing ghillie and deer-stalking pony-man.

Then four months ago he was taken on as a full-time trainee ghillie and gamekeeper. So his cup of joy was full!

And now sitting gazing appreciatively around, glowingly conscious of the great camaraderie uniting all those who shared this boat, his cup seemed to overflow with a happiness un-imaginable back in Glasgow.

With a natural kindliness and that gentle thoughtfulness that made her such a good primary school teacher, Lorna forced her engrossed attention away from Ewan, she turned on the seat and smiled at Duncan.

'You seem very contented there, Duncan. One would almost think you were happy in your new job; were really keen on this interesting new work.'

With perhaps a touch of tolerant reluctance Ewan also turned his thoughts away from his fiancée and the engrossing plans for their forthcoming wedding and honeymoon. He grinned at Duncan with mocking good humour, 'Aye, I have a hellish time trying to keep the young bugger's wild enthusiasm for all his new gamekeeping work under reasonable control!'

With their joyously active tails both dogs silently joined in the loud laughter of the three humans.

As the boat continued its steady way towards the Eastern end of the loch the pleasant May sunshine bathed them in its sensuous glow and revealed all the surrounding mountains with an aesthetic crystal clearness.

As they beached the boat both dogs leapt and eager splashed for welcome shore.

All three humans followed and, not quite so joyously eagerly, started unloading the boat. They then carried its heavy load of large Calor gas cylinders, full jerrycans of petrol, tins of creosote, two rucksacks of food, two sleeping-bags and one indispensable bottle of whisky the one hundred yards to a neat wooden bothy.

Ewan and Duncan were going to spend the next three nights in this comfortable bothy. They would creosote its weathered wooden walls. They would store the gas cylinders and jerrycans of petrol here for future use by this sporting estate's summer fishing parties and autumn deer stalkers. They would *not* leave any of their whisky here!

They planned to do some fishing themselves during the next three days and Duncan was keen to climb one of the surrounding mountains, the only one he had not yet climbed.

Lorna was not going to stay with them. She had to be at work tomorrow morning. She had come to enjoy the trip up the loch and to see this isolated wee bothy set in this lovely, dramatically wild Highland landscape.

She looked forward to spending a few nights here with Ewan sometime, but only after they were married when, as man and wife, they could do so without having to suffer the severe disapproval of her narrowly pious mother.

As Ewan prepared to set off to return Lorna to her car left at the other end of the loch, he instructed, 'Oh, Duncan, you better keep Glen and Rab secure in the bothy with you until we get out of sight down the loch.' He grinned at his dogs who, having heard their names, were alertly listening, 'We don't want you two mad rascals to come swimming after the distant boat again, do we?'

'No, we don't,' Duncan agreed, 'I'll keep them with me while I sort out all the gear in the bothy. Later I'll walk them down the loch shore and meet up with you on your return journey.'

He smiled at Lorna and Ewan, 'And I trust you two love-birds will go straight on down the loch and don't stop somewhere en route to get up to some amorous hanky-panky!'

Lorna laughed as she got settled in the boat huggingly close to Ewan, 'Och, surely you don't really think we would do anything like that, do you, Duncan?'

★ ★ ★

After getting both dogs reluctantly settled on the floor of the bothy, Duncan threw a sleeping-bag on each of the two wooden bunk-beds. He stacked their food away then set the whisky bottle in the place of honour on the middle of the table. He then started connecting up one of the large gas cylinders to the bothy's small cooking stove.

★ ★ ★

As their boat made its steady way back down the loch Lorna and Ewan were soon again wondrously self-engrossed in their wedding plans. Soon they, especially Ewan, became quite erotically excited as they disclosed and frankly discussed each other's inmost thoughts concerning their wedding night and the subsequent nightly delights of their honeymoon.

Their hopefully soon to be realised rosy dreams were suddenly startlingly shattered by a loud explosion.

'What the hell was that?' Ewan gasped.

'It must be a plane that's crashed!'

'Oh but, Lorna, we've not heard any planes for hours; not since these Tornados screamed over early this morning.'

'Then what caused that explosion? Where do you think it happened?' Even as she asked these questions Lorna was overcome by a terrible sickening feeling. She intuitively knew that the explosion had come from the bothy they had so recently left.

Ewan read her agonised thoughts. He solemnly nodded, 'Aye, I'm afraid it did seem to come from about that bothy.'

He swung the boat violently around and thrust the powerful outboard motor into full speed.

Once they cleared a jutting rocky promontory they had a clear view up the length of the loch. Their worse fears were realised. Even from this distance there was no mistaking the flaring fierceness of the flames that seemed to engulf the bothy. And already a thick ugly cloud of black smoke was billowing high above the flames.

Lorna shuddered with terrible dread. Tears overflowed her emotional eyes. 'Oh God, Ewan, what's happened there? What's happened to Duncan, and Glen, and wee Rab?'

Desperately keeping his own shocked emotions under control, Ewan gasped, 'I... I'm afraid it doesn't look good for any of them.'

And soon all their worst fears were terribly realised.

Nothing could now be seen of that neat wee wooden bothy. In its place was nothing but soaring flames and billowing smoke. Despite them desperately searching as close as these appalling flames allowed, they found no trace of Duncan or the two dogs.

As they sat dejectedly slumped together Lorna and Ewan hugged each other's sobbing misery.

Eventually, while he stared at that blazing inferno through quavery tear-distorted eyes, Ewan made a desperate effort to force rational reasoning logic to take over from this awful choking emotion.

He felt sure he knew what had happened at this bothy. There must have been an undetected escape of Calor gas and perhaps of deadly fumes from the old jerrycans of petrol; then all too unaware, Duncan, a non smoker, must have struck a match at the stove as he prepared to make a pot of tea.

Ewan hugged trembling Lorna tighter and offered her – and himself – the only slight consolation he could find.

'Oh at least we must be thankful that poor Duncan and the two dogs did not endure any terrible long suffering pain. Their deaths in that awful explosion must have been instantaneous.'

For many long, tremulous, sobbing moments Lorna did not react to Ewan's compassionate attempt to suggest some faint consolation in the terrible suddenness of these tragic deaths. At last she sadly nodded her agreement. Then, after another tense pause wearily said, 'Oh, but even so these sudden senseless deaths are still terribly cruel, aren't they? Poor Duncan, he was so happy in his new gamekeeping work with you, Ewan. For him this was a dream come true.'

'Aye, I know, Lorna., I know.' Ewan sighed deeply, thoughtfully paused, then said, 'I suppose we should be thankful that poor Duncan did have that dream come true, even if only for these four brief, but really happy months. Many people have life-long dreams that never come true. Yes, at least Duncan *did* have his great dream fully realised before he died!'

Otters Laughter

Three otters wildly play, three animated smudges
coal black against fresh, sun-bright snow;
they carefree slide on flattened bellies
and extended legs;
one after the other they joyous shoot
down their steep, ice smooth chute,
fearless plunge into loch's ice-cold water,
neatly undulate out, breathless eager climb,
then, aquiver with ecstatic bliss,
slide down, plunge in again.
Two otters are cute half-grown youngsters,
the third is their mother;
aglow with maternal pride she admires her hardy, healthy,
happy youngsters and, rejoicing,
joins in their exhilarating play
with a supreme carelessness that equals their swift glissades,
reckless splashes and carefree dashes.

A fourth otter lies motionless, looks on with sullen stare,
haughtily disdains to share in the foolishness
of his mate's ridiculous over-active play.
His grey muzzle shows he's getting gey auld,
his heavy head drowsily nods,
his crescent-moon whiskers glittery droop.
He's content to lie at rest and nostalgic remember
his far-off, careless playful youthful days.

But all that wild intoxicating boundless joy,
all that bouncing, squeaking, whistling
all around him can no longer be disdainful ignored.
Casting aside the dreary role of solemn old patriarchal bore
he condescends to join in all this irresistible riotous play.
Soon all solemnity, all dignified condescension is forgot
and he gives by far the loudest squeals of joy.

Like old man magically become boy, his madly exultant
crazily boisterous playful pleasure
outdoes all that the three others can drum up together
as again and again he high dives hell-for-leather
down this wondrous slippery helter-skelter.

I know that otters cannot laugh,
although they most certainly can grin,
but, sliding, plunging, climbing,
don't those four otters laugh
with the joy of their undulating bodies?

I'm sure that each otter's delighted brain
effortless captures those rippling waves
of soundless laughter
and tremulous quivers with ecstatic rapture.

'Caladh' And Eileen
(Caladh = The Haven)

Caladh, that small wooden house that smiles out across
Inverkirkaig Bay is a true haven, is a magnet that strongly attracts,
that unfailing draws back those true friends who return
to be renewed year after year.
To them Caladh is a bright beckoning light
set in the attractive wild vastness of Assynt,
a place where their own city's ugly vileness
fades and for a happy time is forgot as they carefree walk
and companionably talk over many wild Assynt miles.
Or, gasping, sweating, exultant, they climb Assynt's thrilling
hills, or catch wild, hard-fighting trout in some of its
most remote, semi-secret lochs; or they gasp
with wondrous, nerve-tingling sensuous delight
as a noble Kirkaig salmon sudden rises and eager grabs
their expert cast 'Jock Scott' fly.

Some friends return to Caladh to escape their dreary daily
cycle ride through Rotterdam's ceaseless traffic's vile
polluting fumes, its constant hell
of sulphuric oil refinery smells.

Some leave Glasgow to find a nerve-restoring calm at Caladh
far from where they try to teach unruly youngsters,
try to keep them under reasonable control,
a daily grind that takes a nerve-sapping toll.

Others escape from New York's overcrowded, darkly overshadowed
canyons, from its frantic killing pace,
from that ceaseless competing, that desperate completing
of ever more urgent orders,
from its never-ending crazy hectic race.

Other great friends come from Carlisle, leave for a while
these bypassing motorway miles where they
attend with great medical skills
at that savage 'Motorway Madness,'
that senseless brutal madness that
ceaseless maims and kills.

From such scenes, from cities traffic-choked, despair choked
they come to Caladh, to its brighter life, its brighter hope.
All these many friends hear and obey Eileen and Caladh's
insistent beckoning call;
so eagerly return to Caladh and to Eileen –
small, neatly petite Eileen – the huge loving centre of it all...
How her welcoming hospitable smiles, her sparkling eyes,
her joyous glowing face
reveal her huge inner Beauty,
her great inner Grace.

Swallows

'Duncan Good Enough'

At Achmelvich Duncan was a good friend to many,
was well liked by all the neighbouring crofters,
would willingly join in their mutual crofting labours;
but these crofters, all too well aware of Duncan's
rather rough and ready working methods, thought his
eager efforts more a hindrance than a help.
From painful experience each crofter knew to keep well clear
when Duncan was employing his quite unique,
his quite amazing workmanship.
He would happily furiously hammer in the largest available
nails to join together the very thinnest planks.
When a neighbouring crofter suggested he use his smaller, neater
nails, Duncan would drawl out his invariable slow reply, 'Och, no thanks.
What I've done is good enough!'

On his Achmelvich croft Duncan rented out a modest but and ben
to which one of Scotland's foremost poets returned again and again.
One summer that visitor was pleased to see a new toilet shed
which Duncan proudly declares he's made himself;
but that poet was not so pleased when, rising from
the Elsan seat his unsuspecting, unprotected head
savagely met long, sharp, protruding roof nails.

When the bleeding poet went to his nearest crofter neighbour
for some first aid and sympathy, the only sympathy he got
from wide grinning Pollochan was,
'Och, indeed that would hardly be a fitting poetic end
for the great poet, Norman MacCaig, to be found dead
impaled in Duncan's new toilet shed!'

When Pollochan and Flora later 'point out' the dangers lurking
in that new toilet shed of his, Duncan somewhat peevishly said,
'Och, I know. I've seen MacCaig, I've promised to hammer
flat all the protruding nails. Och, all those summer visitors
are getting sae terrible fussy now. I'm sure that for a' thae
damn tourists my new toilet is more than good enough!'

Poor Duncan's final years were sadly marred by illness,
were darkened by much unforgiving pain.
And when he died his soul, trembling with awe,
approached Heaven's gate and apprehensively waited to learn its fate.
Seeing him there, Saint Peter cried, 'Throw wide the gate!...
Welcome, Duncan, to be an Angel, one of us,
truly, Duncan, you are Good Enough!'

The Sniper
(In memory of Angus (A.K.) MacLeod)
(Italy, 1944)

That lone Highland soldier lay hidden high in arid Italian Hills;
weary of watching that dusty track by that almost dry
mountain stream he dreams of his own native hills;
he brightly visioned these much better, though much wetter
rugged Assynt peaks he had youthful climbed;
he dreamt of his beloved River Kirkaig..
Saw it rushing flooded, saw it spouting high leaping salmon.

There's sudden movements by the silent tracks...
His experienced eye instant goes to rifle's telescopic sight
and index finger freezes on the trigger,
is held poised ready to squeeze.
His breath too is held, all done without conscious thought,
instinctive nerves steady and ready to take a fateful shot.

One German soldier comes clearly into view,
he throws off grey tunic and bends to wash
while the Highland sniper's keen eye and poised rifle
follow his every move.
Rising, that German stands and lets the sun dry him;
how young he seems, how slim his tanned body,
surely he's too young to die?

Aye, he seems a mere youth... but a German youth,
aye, and nae doot a Hitler Youth, a fanatic young Nazi!
That awesome thought tightens on the trigger...
Kill him, do your duty, accurate aiming obey your training!

But no, still you let him go.
You sigh, you rest your burdened head;
you've had too much time to think,
now you wonder would that young German
have been better dead?

But on reflection, you do not regret having spared him.
Oh, but it's a truly awesome God-like responsibility
this cooly deciding a fellow human's fate.
Still, you're pleased that this time you've allowed
compassion to overcome hate.

You thirstily lift your army-issue water-bottle,
eagerly gulp not army-issued water, but strong red wine.
You gulp a silent toast to grand old Khayyam,
you happy drink to his wise love of wine.

Suddenly you think: 'What if tomorrow that young German
has me in his sights; have I signed my own death-warrant?
Or worse- much worse - might I have to bear the heavy guilt
of allowing that German to kill some of my brave comrades?
It's too heavy a burden to contemplate...
Gulp more wine, more and yet more wine!
You grin: this is the story of your life...
Too much time to think,
too little time to drink!

The New Branding-Iron
(A Story)

After lunchtime the rain was, if anything, pouring even heavier than it had poured most of the morning.

The flooded river was visibly rising before the eyes of the two waiting gamekeepers.

Mr. Verey, the wealthy owner of this river and of the vast surrounding West Sutherland sporting estate declared, 'The fishing is hopeless now! Let's head for home.'

His pleasantly smiling white-haired wife agreed, 'Yes, and at least we did very well to bag a brace of salmon each before the river started flooding too badly.'

As his Rolls-Royce entered the local village Mr Verey instructed his chauffeur, 'Drop Mrs. Verey off at the shop, then take me to the estate workshop.'

In his van, obediently following the Rolls-Royce, Charlie, the estate's head-gamekeeper, grinned, 'I hope the bugger doesn't keep us hanging about at the workshop too long. My bloody arthritis is telling me tae get into some dry clothes and tae take a braw big warming dram!'

As both vehicles drove along the village's only street little was to be seen out to the briny West but low, louring grey clouds and gale-driven torrential rain.

Having seen their boss's Rolls-Royce coming towards the workshop, naturally all five of his estate maintenance workers were assiduously busy when he, followed by his two gamekeepers, entered the building.

As Mr. Verey gave them all a smiling greeting his keen gaze swept around the workshop. There was nothing in his estate that did not come under his active, critical scrutiny. He noted with silent approval one worker sawing up firewood and one chopping kindlings then throwing them into sacks ready for delivery to his shooting-lodge. Two others were creosoting fence posts. He addressed the estate foreman, 'Ah, Neil, I see the new branding-iron has arrived. That is what I came in to ask about.'

'Yes, sir, it was delivered only an hour ago. I've just started using it.' Neil pointed to a couple of shovels with his employer's initials, R.A.V. (Ralph Andrews Verey) freshly branded onto their wooden shafts.

'Ah, good, good! That brand will make it clear that those shovels are my property and that they belong to my estate and to no one else, won't it?'

'Yes, sir, it will, it certainly will!' Although Mr. Verey had smiled as he made his remark, Neil felt an implied rebuke behind that smile, sensed an unspoken accusation that he, as foreman, had allowed too many estate tools to 'disappear' over the last few years. The estate factor had let him know that Mr. Verey was complaining of the expense of constantly replacing these missing estate tools and had ordered this new branding-iron in consequence.

As if reading his foreman's thoughts, Mr. Verey again smiled, 'Once all my estate tools are branded they should not 'disappear' so frequently, should they?'

Keeping his annoyance well hidden, Neil returned his boss's smile, 'No, sir, they shouldn't.'

As they discreetly but alertly listened the two waiting gamekeepers exchanged grinning glances. They knew they were both amused by the same thought: how fantastic it was that Mr Verey, a very wealthy business man controlling vast international enterprises, should have got so worked up about the expenses of replacing a few lost estate tools.

Mr. Verey now grabbed the red-hot branding iron and instructed, 'Bring all the tools to me, Neil, and I'll brand them myself,'

As Neil held each shovel, pickaxe, spade and long or short shafted heavy hammers it was expertly branded with the letters R.A.V. by the beaming owner of these initials.

The gamekeepers again exchanged amused glances and Charlie whispered, 'He's as happy as Larry there. He's like a wee boy with a special, "brand" new toy!'

'Aye, it just proves that every man, no matter how wealthy, how busy or important he is, really is still just a wee boy at heart. Or perhaps he thinks he's back when, as a young man learning about the vast family business, he helped brand some of the many thousand cattle they owned in Argentina, Australia and New Zealand.'

Soon all the tools were branded and , still eagerly holding the branding-iron, Mr. Verey looked around for something more to brand.

With his eyes merrily gleaming, Charlie whispered to the estate worker who was bending over chopping kindlings, 'I don't think you should bend ower like that, Norman... you're liable to get R.A.V. branded on your arse!'

Hearing the uncontrollable laughter, Mr. Verey swung round, 'What did you say, Charlie? What's the great joke?'

'Och, sir, I just warned Norman that, bending ower like that, he was in danger o' getting R.A.V. branded on his backside.'

Through his hearty laughter Mr. Verey gasped, 'Oh, Charlie, Charlie, you don't really think I would brand poor Norman, do you?'

'Och no, sir, I don't suppose you would.' Charlie paused and his now silent audience waited expectantly. With his grin getting even wider, he quietly thoughtfully murmured, 'But seeing how much pleasure you were getting from so keenly using that branding-iron, on second thoughts I would not quite put it past you!'

Death

Spots of blood gleam on glittering snow,
they make a clear trail
that accurate follows a fox's track
from where tufts of rabbit's downy fur
and blood stained scuffled snow
tell a simple unmistakable tale.

A tale repeated each night, each day,
of no real import,
no epic drama, just natural savage hunger...
or even mere sport.

But rabbit, with screaming fear,
with cruel splintered bones,
more, much more, to thee
as suddenly the entire Universe ceases to be!

A. K's Last Dram

As ebbing tide drained Inverkirkaig Bay
in those cold dark, pre–dawn January hours
A. K. MacLeod in his crofthouse bedroom overlooking
that draining bay lost his struggle to cling to life
as he gushed a hideous tide of blood.

Four of A. K.s distraught friends –
Norman, Charlie, George and I –
stand in collective sorrow,
share deep despairing sighs
as we lift his lifeless body
and with gentle care ease our burden –
that very heavy burden –
down awkward twisting narrow stairs.

After decently arranging A. K's candle white body
we huddle around with suppressed emotions
then George quiet slipped from this gloomy room.
Soon, armed with badly needed whisky,
he reappears and four well filled glasses
tremble against one another then four urgent drams
gulp a heartfelt silent toast to him,
the focus of all our distraught thoughts,
sadly, untimely dead A. K.

Then did his voice shadow around this dismal room?
Did it indignant ask, 'Where's *my* glass?...
Where's *my* damn big dram?'
All sensed that voice, for, with still
no word being said,
George poured a generous dram
then gently set it by A. K's waxen head.

Sad Bay

Soon after A.K's death two friends who'd been mourners
at his deathbed were, in two cruel tear-filled years
themselves dead.
And now in three grey houses that huddle
around Inverkirkaig Bay
three widows mourn with grief deeper than words can say.
They get some little comfort from shared grief and tears,
from shared memories going back through many years.
Their husbands had been the best of friends
forever sharing drams, songs, honest laughter
and joyous fishing trips that seemed would never end.

Through long, black, winter nights each stricken widow
lay in sleepless grief;
when blackness turns to grey each prays
for this new day to bring some relief;
but still those grey houses, those ancient rocks,
everything in this still lovely bay
seems all shrouded in a duller, sadder grey.

Lonely Cross

Alone, and delighting in being alone,
she wandered exultant on Suilven's grassy summit dome.
She unashamedly rejoiced in the deep pleasure
of having this fantastic mountain to herself,
of sharing with none this precious aesthetic treasure.

Heart and soul are engrossed with sublime thoughts
as, carefree and careless, feeling feathery light,
she floats rather than walks.

Cruelly betrayed by mundane feet
she slips, she falls, she slides,
gathering speed, she helpless tumbles over smooth grass...
grass treacherously wet and dangerously steep.

Screaming, she hurtles through space,
turning and tumbling
she violently smashes...
again hurtles, again smashes
down steep mountain's stonily indifferent face.

Elderly parents, grieving for her, their only child,
request a small cross be placed
at the rough, remote, scree and heather ground
near the base of that lonely hill
which their daughter had loved
and where her grievous smashed body was found.

Charlie Ross, Assynt Estate's head gamekeeper,
undertook that sad task.
With willing strength he carried that pathetic burden,
that small aluminium cross;
carried religion's message of hope.
With gentle reverence set that cross
low on Suilven's steep North West slope.

Many years have passed,
those heart-broken parents are long since dead,
but that small remote cross
still mutely proclaims their tragic loss.

Many climbers 'conquer' Suilven each summer,
but, keeping to the well-marked, well-worn route,
know nothing of that lonely cross
set low on the mountain's
unvisited North Westerly steep.
It is seen only by hunger-driven prowling fox,
by restless wandering deer
and by greedily grazing sheep.

Now that Charlie Ross is also dead
am I the last human to have seen that cross?
Am I the only one who knows where he set it
in remembrance of that tragic death?
I wonder if that small aluminium cross's
lettering is now worn smooth by Assynt's fierce weather;
is it perhaps partly concealed by encroaching heather?

That sad, neglected small cross
must now be almost completely forgot;
may not have had a sympathetic human visitor
for very many years, so let's hope that those few lines
of mine will ensure it will not be entirely forgot.

A Unique Stane

(A Story)

That hardy old gamekeeper Donnie MacLaren was taking Lord Whitney out
to get his first stag on Benmore Deer Forest to the South of Ben Mhor
Assynt. This high and wildly rugged land was Donnie's home-ground, was
where he had stalked for most of his life.

This was Lord Whitney's first time stalking here, although he claimed to
have considerable deer-stalking experience on other Highland estates. Auld
Donnie had secret doots about the truth of this claim.

Although at least fifteen years younger than sixty five year old Donnie, his
Lordship had real trouble keeping up with the amazingly fit old gamekeeper.
This was not so surprising as the hefty younger man was overweight and much
heavier than lean and wiry Donnie. And Lord Whitney's vivid red face and
bloodshot eyes suggested he was rather too fond of strong drink.

This seemed confirmed when, on one of their halts to spy out the rough
hillside ahead of them, heavily sweating Lord Whitney produced a large silver
flask from his tweed jacket's 'poachers pocket' and eagerly gulped a large
reviving dram. He replaced the flask without offering it to Donnie or to the
gillie with them. These two Highlanders licked parched lips and exchanged
secret meaningful glances. These experienced men came to the same unspoken
conclusion: He might be a Lord, but, by God, he certainly was no real
gentleman!

No, he definitely was not like the real old aristocratic landed gentry they
usually took stalking. These real gentry were strict traditionalists who made a
point of giving their gamekeepers and ghillies a dram before they took one
themselves. They did this even knowing that sometimes, if there were a
number of gamekeepers and ghillies and their flask was not large, after it had
passed around these eager gulping Highlanders there was not much whisky left
for the (usually) resigned and amused gentleman.

Donnie thought that Lord Whitney's clothes also revealed the fact that he
was not real gentry. Although obviously expensive and of first rate quality his
tweed jacket and matching plus-fours seemed far too immaculately new and

their checks much too broad and bright. And if he, Donnie, thought his Lordship's tweeds much too vulgarly pretentious, how much more must the real gentry think this. There certainly never was anything in the least new, bright or pretentious in the old – sometimes almost ancient – faded and darned tweeds they wore.

After profusely sweating as he tried to keep up with Donnie coming up this steep hill, Lord Whitney, despite his reviving whisky, now shivered in the cool North Westerly September wind as he lay resting while Donnie thoroughly scanned the surrounding shaded corries and high, sun-catching heathery ridges for deer,

Somewhat impatiently and peevishly Lord Whitney asked, 'Well, MacLaren, do you see any stags?'

'Oh aye, my lord, there are a puckle o' fine stags over on Sgonnan Mhor there.'

'Where?... Where?... Show me!... Show me!'

Through his powerful binoculars Lord Whitney inspected the stags Donnie had spied with his telescope.

'Ah yes, I see some good stags there. Is that biggest one a twelve pointer, a "Royal"?'

Donnie had already counted the points on its antlers. 'Och no, its a ten pointer. It's a fine beast for ye tae bag.'

'Only a ten pointer, eh? I am keen to bag a "Royal",' his Lordship petulantly replied. 'Can you not see a "Royal" for me anywhere, MacLaren?' Donnie *had* spied a "Royal" in another small herd of stags higher up the hill, but he was not going to disclose that grand, much sought after stalking prize to his Lordship. He vindictively though: Och, nae doot ye are keen tae bag a "Royal", but a noble "Royal's" far tae good a stag for a whisky miserable bugger like you!'

With a bad grace he did not bother to hide, Lord Whitney agreed to go after the ten pointer stag. 'All right, MacLaren, let's get going. I'm getting dashed cold sitting here. If I go down through that corrie then up that next small ridge I will get within rifle range of my stag, won't I?'

As Lord Whitney started to get to his feet, Donnie commanded, 'Haud on a minute, my lord. Sit doon again. There's a wee bit o' a snag wi your plan tae get within range o' yon stag.'

'Oh, what's the matter now, MacLaren? I want to bag my stag and not sit freezing here all day!'

With an effort Donnie kept his temper under control. But he was getting damned sick of this Noble Lord. Or this not so noble lord. Suddenly he remembered hearing some of the real gentry disparagingly talk about the many bloated war profiteers who, by gifting lavish sums to Lloyd George's Liberal Party in time for the 1919 General Election, had been given titles. So many of those new Peers had made their obscene war profits from their breweries and distilleries supplying the British Army and Royal Navy with all their beer, rum and whisky during the entire First World War that these upstarts were not referred to by the old true gentry as having been elevated to The Peerage, but having been deviously elevated to 'The Beerage'. This damn bugger, Lord Whitney, must be wan o' thae obnoxious 'Beerage!'

'Aye,' Donnie now repeated, 'there's a real snag wi' your plan. See whit's on yon wee ridge ye meant to go to?'

'What's on that ridge, MacLaren? I don't see anything.'

'No, perhaps ye don't, but I see an auld hind, an alert "Auld Dowager", lying there. She would soon see us an' her alarmed bark wid scare thae stags away.'

'Where is this old hind you see? I cannot see her.'

Donnie pointed her out and Lord Whitney stared through his binoculars. 'Oh I think you're making a mistake, MacLaren. That's just a large stone on that ridge there.'

'A stane, is it, my lord? Well I've stalked ower this land for damn near forty years an' I've never seen a stane like that before. It's a gey queer stane!'

'Oh, damn it, man, what are you talking about?'

'Weel, my lord, it's the first time I've ever seen a stane waggin' its lugs!'

Charlie's Rowans
(In memory of Charlie Ross)

As Charlie sets out from Inveruplan on his autumnal
game-keeping rounds he plucks a handful of rowan berries,
thrusts them in his tweed jacket's deep pocket;
long before ecology became the 'in thing'
he with these berries helped single-handed
enhance this barren Assynt land.

His gamekeeper's beat is vast, is wild and rugged,
stretches from flooding River Inver's peat-stained estuary
to Canisp's lonely, stark and stony summit.
This is a land of neglect, a gale-scoured landscape
of gnarled struggling heather, of bottomless black bogs,
of age-convoluted rocks.
Its ancient tree cover is long since gone...
Lost at what a cost of impoverished soil,
of poor, acidulously soured heather moors.

How sturdily Charlie strides over this familiar ground,
this untamed, overgrazed, sadly maimed land,
how purposefully he seeks out small sheer cliffs
or deep, storm-gashed, burn-splashed miniature ravines
or precariously steep, rock-scattered scree slopes.
He drops rowan berries in rocky cracks and gaping fissures...
Cracks and gaps inaccessible to ever-hungry
ever-searching sheep and deer.

Each berry is a bright red fertile hope which,
with time, with luck, will flamboyant brighten
these mineral-depleted barren hills.
He throws berries on to the curly heather wig
which cosily fits and enhances the stone cold scalp
of a massive boulder.
There, in a few years, ferocious struggling rowans appear;
they send up tiny fragile shoots,
they uncurl desperately delicate green leaves.
There's amazing strength in these thread-thin rowan roots
which assiduously insist their way through a maze
of hair-line cracks and – dauntless adventures –
force dangerous dark passages
and discover strange new routes.
In time those mighty, ever expanding, ever exploring roots
will shoulder that mighty boulder assunder.

I again think of that man of vision
who seemed just an insignificant speck
in that vast landscape of neglect
but who, fulfilling a self-imposed mission,
in real, if modest, measure
helped redress some of Assynt's grievous tree loss
and I, eagerly plucking and selectively dispersing my
rowan berries, humbly followed
the wise example of Charlie Ross.

Rebirth

Back here after some absent years
I again walk the Glen Canisp track.
Although my feet are not quite so fleet
they keep keenly steadily going
while, sweating and gasping, I think that
never before were these parts of this track
just quite so damned steep!

Then, like a mirage, a new Suileag sudden appears.
I am amazed to see that house reborn;
gone are the rusty remains of its decrepit tin roof;
it is no longer a derelict wreck, all sadly forlorn,
now, once more, it is soundly snugly weather-proof.

New windows refuse entry to gale-driven rain,
with fresh-glazed glittery eyes they gaze
with reborn pride across the wide glen
to steep, stolidly solid unchanging old Suilven.
Stout new doors deny entry to plaintive complaining sheep
which had often rested on derelict Suileag's rotting floors.

Suileag, so recently and so neatly renovated,
is now a most welcome sight,
is a cheerily welcoming climber's bothy.
I am delighted that that old house
will not follow the all too many remote Assynt homes
which have decayed to nothing
but gaunt gables and a sad rickle of cold grey stones.

Climbing Suilven

How fine and grand it is to again stride
Glen Canisp track's familiar lovely lonely miles
in the azure pure promise of this May morn's fresh dawn.
With what fine quixotic fun the peeping sun
sends its noble lances to challenge, then vanquish
the cloying, clinging, creamy mist that insistent
smothers that belatedly benighted drowsy giant, Suilven.

Slowly, reluctantly, morning's heat-promising mist clears
and Suilven's full magic majesty appears,
and, as always, this isolated mountain effortless dominates
this vast, wild, Assynt landscape.

As morning's increasing strength of light gets hazeless purer
the cloudless May sky gets more azure blue
and I advance with a stride that seems made
effortless by a touch of re-born youthful vigour.

As I pass Loch-na-Bearraig I have many happy memories
of its fine, wild fighting, speckled trout,
and I again think of how hardy were these Highlanders
who lived in that wee bothy whose overgrown outline
can still be seen beside that attractive wee loch
and who climbed each day to build that massive dyke
that still bestrides Suilven's narrow Western ridge.

Soon my youthful-seeming eager feet are thumping up
the large, well-worn natural steps that lead up this
steep mountainside's giant stairway;
soon I pass through the age-worn gap in that thick dyke
and scramble up the final, well-marked summit track.

Before taking my ease at the summit cairn
I stand and stare and gain immense happiness as I thrill
to the beauty of Assynt's near and distant majestic hills;
then I note the verdant vividness of Elphin's limestone greens,
then delight to see the sparkling glitter where Veyatie Burn
rushes, tumbles and gushes into the serpentine twists and turns
of Fion Loch's trout-rich Eastern reaches
while, further South, huge Loch Sionascaig proud floats
its load of tree-cloaked islands.

With these and many other large lochs and countless lochans
there is as much fresh water as rugged, peat-soured Assynt land,
and out there to the West beyond the glittering Minch
there is a smudged pencil line that must be
the famed, haze hidden distant Hebrides.
All around there is perfect calm and peace as ancient Suilven
heedless dominates over Assynt's glacier-gauged glens
and patient waits for an Ice Age to return again.
Meanwhile I - not quite so ancient, not quite to indifferent -
patiently and contentedly look on while May's joyous sunshine
glows my face and tells me that each brief human life can be -
as mine's these precious minutes is - truly fine and grand

Gneiss Philosophy

Our weary feet falter then halt, our labouring lungs gasp,
our amazed eyes gape;
our awed minds are almost overwhelmed by this remote
Assynt place's encircling waste of sad grey rock.
Ponderously heavy slabs of Lewisian Gneiss lay the weary weight
of their three billion years over this achingly ancient place,
this savage contorted primordial land of unrelieved rock
and evil deeps of blackest peat.

As an oozily eager squelchy peat bog grabs our feet
these immense slabs of grey rock seen to stealthy stalk
and insistent thrust the intolerable burden
of their three billion years at us.
This Gneiss, this solid mass of petrified time,
has been created by more fabulously fantastic forces,
has existed through far vaster oceans of time
than was dreamt of in the simple creation of Genesis.

We weak, vulnerable, petty humans feel grievous crushed
under the appalling dormant weight of these vast slabs of rock;
what human philosophy can reassure us,
can answer the profound questions so weightily raised
by those awesome symbols of vast aeons of time
which were incredibly ancient long before the first hint
of higher life wriggled trembling from the first primeval slime.

And yet, standing gaping, we are not completely overwhelmed,
are not entirely crushed under the grinding shudder
of all this solidified thunder.
We, perhaps foolishly, trembling think we feel these grey slabs
insistent demand that we urgent grab our brief blink of time,
thankfully take all that Life can give,
let blossom whatever creative gifts we have been blessed with.

One Horse Power

Dry Fly Fishing

Great is that heart thumping thrill when a large salmon
eager grabs your slyly attractive deceptive fly;
wildly exhilarating is that salmon's mad unstoppable rush
that sets your line hissing in keen pursuit and makes your blurring reel
sing out its mad, nerve-tingling scream.

Wondrous is that sea-trout's high, half seen leap
through dusk's mysteriously dim half-light,
clear heard is each violently repeated splash...
They flash your nerves back many years
and you hear the triumphant shouts of your hunting/fishing ancestors.

But perhaps an even greater thrill that these great fishing thrills
are the more gentle, more quietly attractive delights
of dry fly fishing for large, plump, wild golden trout
is one of Assynt's high, remote, almost secret lochs
where, under the spell of June's calm clear azure sky,
we see the first May Fly of this new season rise...
Eager rise then sedately sail until delicately
sipped down by a large trout.

We eager mark that gentle rising trout as our special target;
we cautious stalk nearer; as we get within casting distance
our nerves subtly thrill as we bring our utmost fishing skills
into play and try to outwit that wise old trout's
inbred caution.

We succeed! That skilfully deceived trout gently sucks down
our imitation May Fly.
We apply pressure, we must keep that trout
from that thick patch of water weeds.
Apply too much pressure and we'll snap our fine line,
too little pressure and we'll lose that strong surging trout
in these weeds or these high vertical reeds.

Our Dry Fly fishing skills are eventually well rewarded.
We admire and almost shamelessly gloat over the beauty
this large, plump, red freckled golden trout retains
even in death.
We, almost drooling, can almost taste the succulence
of its well cooked firm pink flesh.
It's easy to guess how our hungry ancestors felt as they,
with their much less delicately fine fishing skills,
caught similar trout in this or similar Assynt Lochs
amongst these ancient unchanged Assynt Hills.

Stoer Point

After leaving Lochinver that Fraserburgh fishing boat
butted its bow Northward through the Minch,
was soon fishing daringly near to Stoer Point's
sheer sandstone cliffs.
Perhaps the all too alluring siren call of this
jutting point's fish-rich waters overcame
experience's wise caution;
perhaps a sudden, unexpected tidal surge
or perhaps some sudden fantastic howling gust
from around this weather-contorting point
drove that boat to sudden grief
on a razor-sharp lurking reef.

That savagely smashed boat quickly foundered,
the entire crew drowned.
Stoer Point's treacherous seas seemed to sadistically gloat
as they took their own cruel time before they loosed
their vile grip on their playthings –
those cruelly battered, hideously bloated fishermen's bodies.
Slowly, oh so amazingly slowly, the imperceptibly
healing years passed;
one young widow's grieving tears gradually dried,
her fisherman husband had died on that boat at Stoer Point;
now she re-married, her second husband also a Fraserburgh fisherman.
For some quiet contented years he too fished out from Lochinver,
then, again suddenly inexplicably, his boat also came to grief
on those same deadly lurking reefs at Stoer Point.
Once more the entire crew drowned...
Once more that terrible, devastating, torturing wait
until the bodies are found...
Once more that hideous harrowing ordeal
of trying to identify the obscenely maimed remains.

That inconsolable young widow had never seen Stoer Point,
refusing to be dissuaded, she determined to see this fatal place.
Many distraught eyes follow her firm thrown dark green wreath
as it erratic glides down from these high cliffs
to meet these cruel surging seas where both her husbands had
drowned.
Then all turn and leave that solitary wreath
to express their deep felt grief.

Not only those who come by sea to Stoer Point
are at risk, for these formidable sheer cliffs
seem to lie in wait with malevolent intent,
seem almost gloatingly eager to fling any foolish overconfident
human to a terrible screaming death.

One such death came to one young man as a friend and he
joyous explore above the sheer drop at the Old Man of Stoer.
These friends excited gasp at seeing how that vertical stack
thrusts up its amazing sandstone exclamation mark.
Betrayed by careless foot, one stumbles then hurtles...
Terrified screams as he falls through space...
Violent splashes into this malicious place's
evil seething seas.
No intuitive sense or guess tells his young wife
that she is now a widow, nor that her chuckling
chubby baby is now fatherless.

Even for those plunged into darkest grief the slow passing years
eventually, mercifully, bring some relief;
grief's thrusting torturing blade must slowly rust
or Life could not go on...
gloating Death would be too atrociously victorious.

And so even the saddest memories of Stoer Point's tragic tales
gradually pale; some even dare to think its seeming
malignant mysterious powers are at last at rest.
And then these mysterious evil powers strike again...
they take the lives of two young local men...
they make it worse by these fine young men being brothers.
Experienced aqualung divers, these brothers have often
explored and fished around Stoer Point's familiar waters.
Probably one brother got into difficulties,
probably the other bravely went to his aid;
together they must have desperately struggled,
together they must have tragically died.
These tragic deaths forge a terrible chain of grief,
an unbreakable chain of almost unbearable pain
that links one young widow and her fatherless children
to desolate parents, grandparents and many overwhelmed friends.

Many desperate desolate years draggingly pass
and, as Stoer Point claims no further victims,
some again foolishly wonder if these un-quiet seas
have found calm peace at last.
But those who best know its cruel history,
who have tried to guess its unfathomed mystery,
feel sure of one thing...
that, in years to come, the inscrutable Point of Stoer
will insatiably claim some more.

Footnote:
Since the above poem was written the Point of Stoer has claimed some more!
In July, 2007 a young man and woman were swept to their deaths as they were
taking photos of its wild seas surging up a steep shelf of rock.

No Heathcliff Me!

Assisted by a gentle nurse she timorously advances
down the hospital's long corridor.
The smiling nurse pointed me out to her
as I advanced from a different door.
She lifted her bowed head and stared like one sudden entranced
then held out eager, wasted, trembling hands.

No young Cathy, all wind-blown raven locks she;
ageing, balding, bespectacled, no rugged passionate Heathcliff me!
I smile to hide emotions sudden tears;
for an everlasting minute we embrace
and happiness transforms her illness withered face.
Our entwined souls soar, return to a happier place...
Not to the Brontë's immortal Yorkshire moors
but to Assynt's higher wilder hills and moors,
that windswept landscape we both had loved
with a love deep and sure.
For that precious long minute
we roll back time's all too greedy years.

Trapped Butterfly

That trapped butterfly ceaseless flutters
its desperate struggle to be free;
incomprehensible is this invisible barrier
that keeps it trapped,
keeps it away from breezy summer air
where it belongs, where it longs to be.
Trapped in wide gap in that double-glazing
amateurishly set in small cottage hospital's
thick old grey walls, that fluttering butterfly
is all too obviously symbolic
of all those other fluttering souls
trapped in this geriatric ward.

How desperately all these unseen souls trapped
in tenacious grip of age-withered flesh
try to struggle free...
Try to soar with that freed butterfly
and gain their future bright immensity.

Watching

Awaiting her approaching end, I watch
through sleepless nights, through exhausting days.
Trying to whisper some comfort, I mumble some
inarticulate vaguely hopeful prayers.
Through deep depths of grief I watch her lying there
and suffer with her suffering as she bravely struggles
to keep relentless death at bay.

Then, sudden feeling utterly tranquil, I seem to gentle rise,
seem to leave my body, seem to serenely hover
and, gazing down, seem to clearly see this
hushed hospital scene.
I see with vision inexplicable, see realms beyond pain,
realms that seem beyond the brain,
fantastic realms where calm reason's normal logic
would fear to go.

I see with vision crystal bright, a seeming mystic vision
that lets me see from some higher plane;
lets me see me sitting there watching her,
and then, seeming from some even stranger higher layer
of vision, this higher self keen watches
my other hovering self watch me sitting watching her.

Later, looking back with logic's calm reasoning brain,
it seems abundantly clear that all that fantastic
hovering and higher watching can easily be explained
as a hallucinatory escape...
An understandable temporary escape from long lasting
stress's overwhelming strain.

Oh but how gloriously bright, how pure crystal clear,
how flaringly vivid were these levitating visions,
how much deeper, clearer, keener than anything seen
by normal everyday life's un-visionary sight!

Memories

I hold her gently while she babbles confused incoherent words
and tries to articulate past pleasant memories;
some individual words send messages flashing to me,
memories of shared happy times that used to be.
For a brief bright while such glowing smiles
radiate her joyous face as the closed vaults of her mind
unlock and send golden treasures tumbling out.
Such shining eyes smiling into mine
reveal her precious inner find..
Sudden clear memories of a much happier place,
wondrous memories of a much happier time.

'Chico, Dear!'

As I held her wasted, brown blotched hand
in this dim shrouded silent place,
this the night nurses familiar land,
she spoke her last words distinct and clear,
'Chico, dear!'

Chico, her little white poodle,
is many years dead,
but is still alive in her sad, tormented,
but still brightly loving head.

Later, in the dismal hour of false dawn
when all life is at its lowest ebb,
that time those gentle caring nurses most dread,
she gave one quiet gasping sigh –
was dead!
Yet she too lives on
bright within my remembering loving head.

Illusions?

What if after death there is nothing?
Nothing but a complete blank nothing?
A blankness that proves all religious after life promises
to be nothing but a false hollow show.

Still, believers have the best of all worlds;
in life are buoyed by their faith,
after death are spared dread disillusion,
for if all is utter blankness
that blankness is impossible to know.

Goodness, it's almost as though
some kind God
has neatly arranged things so!

PART THREE

Some Pitlochry Years

A Different Landscape

Now alone, I decide to live out my remaining life
amidst the tree-rich verdant lushness
of the Perthshire countryside around Pitlochry.

Although this Pitlochry landscape is much less
starkly dramatic than that familiar wild Assynt land
Eileen and me had lived in for many happy years,
although it does not have any hills quite so dramatically
steeply awesome as Assynt's fantastic Suilven,
does not have Assynt's vividly visible
stark, age-contorted rocks,
still Perthshire does have oh how many more
much taller, stronger, nobler trees
than Assynt's oh so few poor, wind-distorted stunted trees.

How calmly mild is this Perthshire landscape
compared to Assyn't stormy wildness.
I certainly am not sorry to leave behind
its dreadful winters all too familiar
almost hurricane force howling gales,
nor its all too frequent almost horizontal rains
that drive in from the vast, storm mad Atlantic.

Here, quietly contentedly, I will live out my remaining life,
will be quietly grateful for the more gentle bliss
this Perthshire landscapes gives;
will be deeply thankful for the blessed balm
of this quiet place's well sheltered calm,
its gale-lessness and – compared to Assynt – its almost rain-lessness!

Yes, I will joyous explore and quickly get to know
much more of this blissful Pitlochry district than we knew
as occasional casual passing Summer visitors.

'The Fairest Portion'

'Perthshire - the fairest portion of the Northern Kingdom'
From The Fair Maid of Perth by Sir Walter Scott

Just as almost without doubt Perthshire *is* truly
'the fairest portion' of this ancient land,
so surely the area around Pitlochry *is* Perthshire's
'foremost part', well blessed with natural glories
that uplift many sad, city-jaded hearts.
How gladly verdantly lushly is this place clad
with countless brave, mature, varied trees;
how many 'minor' hills rise so splendidly invitingly
from so many gentle flowing heather moors
while these noble rivers rush and flood
through awesome ravines and urgent foam over impeding rocks
until tamed by Pitlochry's own, man-made loch.
Faskally and other large lochs boldly alluringly
stretch out their impressive lengths while some smaller lochs
stay demurely hidden, but even the most modest
of lochans, once seen, is never quite forgotten.

All Pitlochry's surroundings resonate with beauty...
Beauty that ever changes with the changing seasons.
Many thrilled and excited visitors astounded gaze around
and agree that Golden Autumn is this district's
fairest season, the one that wears the noblest crown
and makes this part of Perthshire a place apart...
A place ever glowing bright in every alertly receptive heart.

It's a Jungle Out There!

Just as we surmise that it would not be wise
to get between a herd of thirsty African buffaloes
and their eagerly sought watering hole
so likewise in Pitlochry it is most unwise
to get between a herd of trippers disgorging from
their touring bus and the nearest tea-room.

Urgent is that rush for tea,
frantic the quest for toilets!
In that eager race they forget
to be sedate...
They lose all lady-like grace!
Those dear old white-haired ladies thole
no delay; if you get in their way,
impede them en-route for tea,
or even worse, en route for relief,
you are liable to come to grief...
are likely to be ruthless tramped underfoot!

Hearty Breakfast

Taking my dog on pre breakfast stroll by Faskally's
tree-lined caravan park I pass many caravans
all alive with breakfast hustle.
They all waft delicious smells of frying bacon;
such tempting scents, such unkindness to so cruelly
remind me of my waiting healthy breakfast.
Somehow the though of all-bran and muesli
definitely palls, insipid, unappetising,
does not appeal at all!

We pause behind one especially odorous caravan;
the smells, the sounds, glorifying from spluttering frying-pan
make my senses flip...
I feel as if on a drug-induced 'trip'.
Foolishly grinning, I wolfish sniff each whiff,
inhaling deeply, I'm transmuted to being a 'Bisto Kid'.
My poor frustrated dog looks on, he too keenly sniffs,
he too licks cruelly deprived drooling lips!

My overpowered senses now reel out of hand,
such temptations are more than flesh and blood can stand.
Taking the shortest route we rush to caravan park's shop,
we urgently load up with sausages, black-pudding,
succulent bacon, and for this once to Hell —-
to the very Devil -
with any concern for my cholesterol level!

Wee Craigower

Oh neat, steep, petite Wee Craigower
despite your modest height
you boast some fabulous views,
proud views infinitely greater
than many a higher but duller 'Munro' can show.

Loch Dunmore

Loch Dunmore is hardly large enough to be termed
a true loch, is hardly even a true lochan,
is little more than an artificial man-made pond.
Man-made, but after many years transformed
by Nature's magic wand to a place of true beauty.
A place where Larch and Birch display Spring's
tenderest sheen and give promise of Summer's
maturing green.

In due season the Rhododendrons blushing flowers
vivid brighten their sombre leaves
and with their varied short-lived hues
marvel at clear June sky's delicate eggshell blues.

Then sharp Iris leaves dagger vertically up,
stab through insect-humming drowsy air,
lead the way for their flowers buttercup yellow brightness
to follow and add their additional beauty
to the magnificent beauty already there.

Now on their large green saucers Water Lilies
place elegant sets of bright white cups;
this peaceful scene is made perfect
as maternal Mallards proudly watch their darting ducklings
as they eager quest and sup around these floating cups.

Giant old Scots Pines spread their high canopies
and glow their magnificent purplish–green shine
while in secluded bays elegantly slim Birches –
the 'Silver Ladies' of the woods – lean over calm water
to coyly admire their own Summer bright reflections.
All this to be seen at Loch Dunmore, this one small lochan
that with its ever varied beauty is beautiful at any time,
but when flaring aflame with Autumn's brilliant glory
then its beauty is truly sublime.

Loch Dunmore

Black Castle of Moulin

This desolate ruin is all that now remains
of the Black Castle of Moulin,
the skeletons of its past are covered
by its fallen, gunpowdered walls
that succeeded in keeping the Plague –
that dreaded Black Death –
from further spreading its obnoxious breath.
Now these fallen ancient walls are deep buried
under five centuries accumulated soil.

A few gauntly precarious, sadly maimed, remnant walls
manage to linger on and pretend to defend
the Castle's centre where there are now massed ranks
not of wild, bloodthirsty, Highland Clans,
but of nothing wilder than a large army
of vicious stinging nettles.

This massed botanic army of verdant bright lushness
is a perfect feeding and breeding paradise for whole
squadrons of palette bright Butterflies.
Here they indulge their mad display of ceaseless dazzling flight,
here they madly flutterly meet, then passionately urgently mate.

Here these kaleidoscopic swarms of gaudily varied Butterflies
careless hovering rise, then fearless fluttering fall,
how effortlessly these radiant rainbowed forms
majestically transform this Black Castle
as they magically flutter away all memories of grim death
and all fears of ugly disease.

As, glorying in the glorious Summer breeze,
these Butterflies cleanse with fluttering ease
Moulin Castle is a place reborn...
Is a place vividly alive with
Butterfly Bright Summery Delight.

Swan Drinking

Standing at lochside your neck stretches stiffly out,
your beak dips, you gently sip cool refreshing water,
then long neck is held poker straight,
is raised high while water oh so slowly
dribbles down your thirsty throat.

This seems such a labourious way to drink,
seems so awkward beside your mate's effortless grace
as her floating beauty is doubled by reflections link.
Then I think, giving a chuckle and an inward laugh,
'Oh you oh so slowly drinking swan
just be thankful you are not a giraffe!'

Crusader

That age and weather smoothed Crusader's gravestone
lies flat in Moulin's ancient kirkyard,
that large, shallow carved sword
proclaims one who fought on what he thought
was a righteous cause.
With keen sword firm in strong hand
he had vainly tried to free the Holy Land.

Would not that keen sword been put to better use,
like brave Wallace, like victorious Bruce,
fighting for Scotland's freedom?
Been better used against fierce, proud, English invaders...
Surely then a truer nobler Crusader!

Pitlochry War Memorial

Of all those many Summer visitors who sit in this
bright public garden very few think of those who
went bravely out into Death's dark night,
those whose names are remembered here, black-embossed
clear against granite's silvery gloss,
names that perpetually commemorate this district's grievous loss...
Those who gave up their right to fun,
who lost their rightful place in the sun.

Younger generations sit and careless gulp 'Coke',
engrossed with noisy laughter and thoughtless jokes
they know nothing of that generation who gave all,
who forfeited Life's brightest joys, its noblest hopes.
Is it only us old enough to remember the last World War
who can truly feel for that lost generation who died
in the Black Obscenity of the First World War?...
Only us who are so deeply moved by those endless rows
of white war graves that flow wave upon ceaseless wave?

We think of those young shepherds who left their
quiet Perthshire hills – places soon to be bereft of most
human life – who left their weeping bairns and their soon
to be widowed distraught young wives.
So many went from those Highland homes never to return,
hardy men who would never more rejoice in ripening Summer sun,
never more share in another harvest won.
They exchanged their demanding Highland soil –
that soil they inarticulately loved –
for the pitiless madness of filthy Flanders mud.
As, proudly waved and cheered, those brave young Perthshire men

entrained in Pitlochry's small railway station none knew
how terribly few would win through to see this hometown again.
These young Territorial Army soldiers proud wear their
Black Watch kilts and naively think themselves bound for
exciting adventures; almost none have been out of this country,
many have never ventured out of their own county.
Together those great comrades willingly faced many hazards,
together they endured dreary months in Flanders sodden trenches,
then they went 'over the top' together and died together,
mere cannon-fodder...
So many bright young lives so culpably ended!

From comfortably remote headquarters had issued decisions
that translated into a deadly spate –
a ceaseless flood of spilling British blood.
So many young soldiers ruthlessly mown down by machine-guns
which kill with efficient mechanical skill...
methodical maniac killings with unfeeling
slaughterhouse precision.

Those many British dead are victims of a hidebound
British General's entrenched mind,
a cavalry officer who thought of wars fought
with sword and lance, an officer blind to all reason,
to all compassion, as he orders yet more futile,
blindly suicidal attacks.
His victims are slaughtered by storms of bullets,
vicious bullets that with savage glee turn humans
into grotesquely torn puppets...
puppets whose legs unavailing kick,
who's hands vainly claw, who's blood-dripping arms
spasmodic jerk as they dangle atrociously brambled
on barb-wire's savage spikes.

Fortunate are those with bright arterial blood pouring...
they quickly died;
tragic are those with lesser wounds who,
hanging entangled in barbed wires ruthless grip
take so terribly long to die...
how awful is all their urgent imploring,
how vicious is all their foul swearing,
but all those prayers to a seeming uncaring God
and all that Devilish cursing and swearing
are all equally unavailing.

Many other of our tragic wounded drown in the watery Hell
of rain-filled shell holes, while yet more fall and flounder
in that foul quagmire of artillery-churned mud...
there, gasping and weeping, they end up fathoms deep
in that inescapable insatiable Flanders mud,
that alien sea of mud that greedily gulped
an entire generations blood.

Truly it would be a desperate shame if all those named
on Pitlochry's War Memorial – all those who fought and died –
should be completely forgot,
should never be paid the tribute
of an occasional sad sighing silent thought.

Pitlochry War Memorial

On Craigower

Happily passing a Summer hour on steep Craigower's
pleasant summit I reflect on this modest hill's warlike past;
there had been fierce tribal battles fought
around this hill's ancient Pictish Fort.

In later centuries Craigower was crowned with a warning beacon.
Alertly manned by local clans, that beacon had often flared,
had flamed alarm's urgent call to arms,
gave dire warning of approaching armies
or of marauding enemy clans.

The many who now ascend this hill climb simply for pleasure;
glorying in enticing views they feel renewed,
find contentment beyond measure.
I, and many others, find this hill so restful,
are thankful that all these past killings have ceased,
that there is nothing now to disturb this hill's perfect peace.
I happily think that Man has at last made
some little, some most welcome progress.

Then suddenly, ferociously, shatteringly, two Tornado
warplanes scream by below this hill.
These startlingly sinister arrow-head shapes
vanish in a few seconds, are immediately out of sight
behind neighbouring concealing heights,
but they leave thunderous polluting noises
uglifyingly lingering behind.

These warplanes use Craigower's prominent landmark
as a convenient turning point;
following the ancient route they go by Loch Tummel
and Loch Rannoch to the West.
Flying so furiously fast, so dangerously low,
these obscenely screaming jets smash through
what was a lovely peaceful glen,
and now, with a rueful smile, I hastily revise
my thoughts on the Progress of Men!

Hazel Stick

That Wild Honeysuckle grows where the light fades,
it clings tight through this wood's canopied shade,
true to its ancient name of 'Woodbine'
it plaits neat vines in urgent twines
round Hazel's straight slim shaft.
It relentless serpentines up host's vertical length
with ruthless boa-constrictor strength
and restricts and constrains with strangling pain.

That poor Hazel's pure true growth
is sadly deformed into corkscrew spirals,
it is ugly deformed into a false, sick,
Harry Lauder walking stick.

Walking on Water

Bold striding on broad Water-lily leaves
that well-grown Moorhen chick goes chasing
after escaping insects.
Delighting in chase, increasing her pace
she walks right off raft's safe surface.
She sinks, bobs up, gives indignant gasps.
Such a profound lesson taught her...
It's not so easy to walk on water!

Collision

As a pale green Mayfly gently rises from loch's calm surface
the June sunshine glitters its fine translucent wings.
Hidden high in clear ethereal Summer sky
an unseen Skylark sings and with its transcendental song
innocently lulls all to drowsy sleep.
But as always amid Nature's most innocent seeming peace
there lurks the constant threat of death.
That fluttering Mayfly, thinking itself wisely escaping
from hungry Trout, unwittingly puts itself in sight
of water-skimming Swallow.
That keen hunting Swallow alters course,
swerves to intercept that rising Mayfly.

As bird's beak opens in expectant gape a large Trout,
its mouth also wide, rises after that same Mayfly.
There's wild confusion as Trout and Swallow
seem to collide in mid-air!

In a few confusing seconds of blurred vision the gliding Swallow
seems to slide over the Trout which now inelegantly flops back
and splashes a bright explosion...
such a desperate white commotion!

Thinking itself under attack, the Swallow gives
nervous shudders, it almost stalls, almost falls
to loch's violated surface, then thankful again
soars high, again glories through sunbright sky
while from curved wings and forked tail
there trail slipstreams of misty spray which appear
gleaming chandeliers of tiny crystal tears.

The Angels Breath

Each morning that old, white-haired distillery guide
went to work with hurrying stride,
with his dark Murray tartan kilt jauntily swinging;
again sniffs distillery's distinctive scents upwardly winging,
once again deeply breathes that sweet smell,
that familiar glorious smell he knew so well
as it issued from these old buildings – 'The Angels Breath.'
That distinct scent mists the air and pervades the earth;
his ancestral Gaels had mournfully named it so
with deep sorrow at such a wasteful way for Whisky to go.
This constant loss of Whisky evaporating from wooden casks
still saddens him as he goes about his daily tasks.

After forty years of working in this distillery, starting as a mere lad,
that scent, that constant reminder, still makes him sad
as he wistfully thinks of all those drams melting into thin air;
even after all this time it still seems so unfair
as those lost drams are odoriferously swept by breeze
to blacken distillery buildings and darken surrounding trees.
Yes, it yet gives him deep sorrow to see such grand Scotch
end in such a way, to stand by and watch
this precious Whisky meet such a dismal shameful death
as it transforms into that wasteful 'Angels Breath'.

Robertson's Oak

George Robertson of Faskally, fleeing from Culloden's
bloody aftermath, sheltered in old Oaks leafy branches,
stayed hidden until searching enemies had passed.
Did he wonder how many years this tree had grown?...
profoundly thankful for its concealing cover
did he wish it a long life after he was gone?

Little did he think that after two and a half centuries
of further sturdy growth this old Oak would suffer the indignity
of having a sewage works at its roots,
would have the Westerly wind waft a most unpleasant stink.

However he certainly would have approved of how *his* tree
ignores the powerful guff of sewage
and thrives on much more pleasant stuff...
these delicate sweet fumes of distillery's 'Angels Breath.'

As Robertson's ancient Oak has survived for so many centuries
surely we can safely assume
that, being a true Highland tree,
it will continue to thrive for many more years
on those life-enhancing Angelic Whisky Fumes!

Contemporary Literature

Pitlochry Library puts on a brave display
of 'The Best of Contemporary Literature' and so,
encouraged and pleasantly assisted by that
Librarian who has graced this place
through many helpful years, I eagerly browse
to discover what these *best* contemporary
writers have to say to me.
I select highly praised books...
Books lauded as near, or even pure, Genius.

As these volumes are eagerly read, all too often
excited anticipation turns to dismay...
So many novels that are simple awful,
are full of squalid writing, sordid characters
and almost no engrossing plot.
As for most of those modern short stories that tell
no story, they've mostly a dreadful dreary lot!

As for most modern verse, it goes from bad to worse...
Has no words that flow with wonder,
has nothing that inspires and illuminates
with transcendental beauty.
Much modern free verse hardly deserves Poetry's
noble name, is largely an esoteric game,
is mostly a pretentious pose,
is so much dreary chopped up prose!

As regards the contemporary literary scene
I'm now resigned to being a Philistine,
one who deplores those boring modern books
which give me little or no delight.
If this is the *best* of Contemporary Literature
I shudder to think what the *worst* must be like!

Opportunists

Two golfers are on Pitlochry's practise green
both are novices, young and keen;
they repeatedly swipe...
send large tussocks into flight.
Many divots travel far, they fall
equidistant with the ball!

Their strenuous efforts are not all in vain.
opportunist gulls benefit from their faulty aim;
truly these turf-churning golfers do some good,
they provide worm-gobbling gulls with abundant easy food!

Mercy Killing

I sit and watch that myxomatosis infected rabbit
as with bloated head and bulging blinded eyes
it tries to hop, staggers, falls, then crawls
in the terrible confusion of its desperate condition.
As I will myself to give one hard blow of my heavy stick
and inflict a swift mercy killing
I see the silent stealthy movement of a hunting stoat.

With constant swivelling of nervous twitching ears
and forever quivering scent questing nostrils
that rabbit ceaseless tries to compensate for sightless eyes.
Carried waveringly on uncertain breeze the scent of that stoat
sends rabbit into panic – literally into a blind panic!
It blindly dashed, it violent smashed into a drystane dyke,
staggering back, it collapsed into a quivering heap of fear
with that stoat's menace terrifying magnified
by being sensed but being unseen.

As the small merciless menace almost silently slithers near
all hope died, the rabbit lay as though paralysed.
The stoat pounces, blood splatters, throat chokes,
rabbit gives a few final useless bounces.

In sentimental human terms that stoat had done good,
had given a quick clean death, a true mercy killing.
And yet how loudly that rabbit had screamed its protest
at the stoat's efficiently administered sudden death.
That rabbit much preferred the useless clinging to a few
more slow lingering painful days,
a few more long lingering weary nights...
It wished to delay in every way
the terrible finality of Death!

One Horse Power

It's most pleasant to watch that massive Clydesdale,
that gentle giant casually guided by that forester.
Sturdy man and huge horse are both getting old,
with each passing year they plod slightly more slowly
up that dappled track, through that sun-bright glade.
Mingling with Faskally Forest's light and shade
are a noble part of this ancient place's continuous story.

That Clydesdale is one horse power of immense muscled strength
that with seeming effortless ease pulls and heaves
and drags each humbled tree's defeated horizontal length
down bracken slope to wait stacked at track.
Then horse and man slow trudge back uphill.

How firm earth shakes, how squelchy ground quakes
as huge hoofs plod and trudge with steady sturdy gait.
The old forester thins out only selected individual trees;
better, much better, this traditional way with plodding
one horse power than that ugly scene across the loch
where giant machines blitzkrieg the land,
where clanking panzers fell all trees with unsparing
ruthless mechanical hand.

These ugly giant machines black belch their massive power,
loudly proudly proclaim their victory as they leave
entire slopes depleted, desolate, defeated
then boast this as their grand triumphant hour.
Oh how much better that living tradition
of One Horse Power where man and horse combine
as through centuries enshrined to become that perfect team
who work harmoniously together through many a contented,
environmentally friendly forest hour.

Commonwealth Roots
(A Story)

Twenty two year old Canadian, Donald Douglas, was on his first holiday outside Canada. He was spending one month in Scotland. Following up on his internet research, he was discovering more of his ancestral Perthshire roots. It was thrilling to meet other members of the once powerful Douglas Clan.

Like many citizens of Britain's 'Old Commonwealth', Donald still fondly regarded Scotland as 'The Old Country.'

While working in the Canadian Forestry Service amongst the huge Douglas Firs of the magnificent redwood forests of Western Canada, he had been inspired to research his family history and was delighted to discover that his family tree was linked to those majestic trees. Through his maternal grandmother he was distantly related to David Douglas.

It was that Douglas, one of the greatest 19th century botanist and plant-hunters, who had bought the first seeds of these giant Canadian firs to his native Perthshire and had been honoured by having these trees named after him.

As he explored North Perthshire's pleasantly wooded countryside Donald Douglas disparagingly smiled at what the Pitlochry tourist board had described as Scotland's majestic 'Big Tree Country'.

Oh no doubt that was a real cute attractively 'cool' label to lure tourists with, but no way could this miniature landscape compare with the real big tree country of Western Canada. Even Perthshire's tallest tree, appropriately a Douglas Fir, was a mere pygmy compared to the Canadian redwood giants he was familiar with.

But gradually this small, this ancient, 'Mother Country' worked its strange subtle ancestral magic on him. The more he got to know this picturesque districts 'lesser' trees the more he came to feel their gigantic attraction.

Leisurely admiringly he wandered past the rushing waters of the tree-rich Linn of Tummel. At the small, 'cool' Coronation Bridge he cast a searching gaze towards the steep slope that hid McGregor's cave.

The further he pleasantly stravaiged towards the West the more he felt those sparkling rivers with their modest waterfalls, those calm lochs, those sun-dappled hills, those fertile glens with their verdant birches ever more irresistibly entwine their seductive charms around him.

The more he came to know this entrancing Perthshire landscape the more obvious, boastful, and even garish seemed the beauty of his native Canada. That country with its awesome vastness, its limitless wild places, its huge lakes like inland seas and the thrusting jagged might of the Rockies combined in an amazing, mind-blowing grandeur that sent the more sensitive human senses reeling in overwhelmed bewilderment.

Canada's overpowering beauty had none of the subtle charm of this modest Perthshire landscape he was discovering with ever increasingly delight. The lure of this charming countryside was further confirmed when he arrived at the Black Woods of Rannoch. The centuries old Scots Pines that formed this wood were remnants of the Great Forest of Caledonia that had once clad the entire Scottish Highlands.

Donald felt that there was something sublime about the rugged beauty of these ancient trees. Each tree was quite unique. Each one made its brave display of its ragged, gale-tormented branches in its own individual way. How sublimely different were these noble natural Scots Pines from the regimented dull conformity of all massed, man-made conifer forests.

When he discovered a tall, isolated Douglas Fir growing beside an attractive, clear-running wee burn in these Black Woods Donald decided this was a perfect place to camp.

Late that evening, after having eaten, after taking another leisurely stroll around these attractive woods, he squirrelled into his snug sleeping-bag.

As he lay alone he fondly, and rather erotically, though of his girl-friend back in Canada. He longed for her. At last making up his mind, he definitely decided he would ask her to marry him as soon as he returned home. He was confident she would accept him. Together no doubt in due course they would perpetuate his Canadian branch of the Douglas Clan.

High above Donald's head a rising breeze whispered through the Douglas Fir's dark branches and lullabied him to sleep.

He never truly awoke from that deep sleep, for sometime in the depth of the witching hours, that venerably mature Douglas Fir was uprooted and dropped its snapping, crashing, massive crushing weight through Donald's flimsy tent.

Lying crushed in bloodied death Donald Douglas's lifeless arms embraced that Douglas Fir's thick greyish truck as in a final effort to heave it off, or in an equally vain effort at a final desperate act of love.

And so that particular Canadian branch of the Douglas Clan died out – died out root and branch!

Greetings

Passing other hikers I polite say, 'Good day,'
smiling think surely I'm giving my age away
with such a greeting in such an old-fashioned way.
Do those happy young backpackers
(backpackers – such an ugly word!)
perhaps think my politeness rather absurd
as they so nonchalantly reply, 'Hi!'?

Red Admiral

Craigower's pleasant summit seems a strange place to meet
a solitary wandering Red Admiral
so remote from any ocean,
so far from any Soviet fleet.
Resting on blush bright pink heather
his flickering wings semaphore secret signals,
perhaps coded messages of urgent naval matters?
Or is that Red Admiral, that sly old sea-dog,
flashing sexy signals to allure
that charming Painted Lady
now so coyly fluttering by?

Craigower

Not a Munro!
(A 'Munro' = a Scottish mountain over 3000 ft. high)

I meet and cheerily greet a young climber and,
learning that he's recently been in Assynt,
I confidently suggest, 'You would have enjoyed climbing Suilven.'
'Oh no,' he replied, 'I did not waste my time on it...
it's not a Munro!'
I hardly know whether to laugh or weep!
At last, aghast, I gasped, 'Not a Munro?...
no I know it's not, but surely there must be some deep malaise
in any blinkered 'Munro-Bagger' who wilfully ignores
'lesser' hills like that majestically unique steep peak, Suilven,
just because it is not a Munro.'

With disbelief, with something like real grief,
I hear that young climber scorn and disdain
all Assynt hills, all except Ben Mhor Assynt,
the district's only 'real' mountain, its one and only Munro,
the only one worthy of being ticked off his long list
of eager climbed Munros.

I think how sad and mad it is that any young keen climber
should so despise these 'lesser' Assynt hills;
not be seduced by Cul Mor's alluring twin breasts,
not feel deep things subtly expressed by modest Canisp
not seek the pleasures scattered along Quinag's
five-peaked straggling ridge, nor guess what secrets
petite Cul Beag whispers.
And surely it's the absolute height of folly
for any 'Munro-Bagger' to ignore the stark sandstone stacks,
the jagged hedgehog bristles of endearing wee Stack Polly.

As I doleful watch that sadly misguided young climber go
I think of him remorseless seeking only his higher hills
and, recalling past climbs on those smaller,
but definitely not lesser Assynt hills,
I wonder how one such as he can ever hope to really know
or truly love our Scottish Hills
when he only knows the Munros.

Roe Deer Fawns

A few moments seen then vanish into Summer's dappled green...
were they real or something of a Mid-Summer dream?
Far more graceful than any ballet star
those twin fawns flow after leaping doe.
Glorying in their effortless beauty they pass
forest's narrow path with one smooth bound...
with neat black hoofs that seem to disdain
dull mundane ground.

Youthful Immortality

This neat new teak seat set high on this hill's
most wearying steep invites to welcome rest
while it mutely proclaims its lasting tribute
from a grieving mother to a tragic departed son.
Aglow with youthful vigour, her son had often
gained the summit of this, Pitlochry's nearest modest peak.

As glowing lads and lassies sit at ease
these sweating young climbers neither read
nor heed that commemorative plague
set at their backs.
They grab a short rest, they briefly admire
this seat's 'real cool' view
before rushing on to urgent seek
then triumphant reach the top
of this Perthshire peak.

Brimful of Youthful Immortality, these youngsters were blind
to the poignant message spelled out clear on damp grass
at that commemorative seat.
That porridge splash of rain-sodden human ash
was an unheeded reminder of the inescapable fact
that all those rushing lads and lassies must
sooner or later all – like Shakespear's chimney-sweepers–
come to dust.

Inheritance

The greatest gift we inherit from parents is health...
health not wealth;
health from healthy parents whom us begat...
and, what's more, there's no tax on that!

Vital Harvest

Some Pitlochry residents see with dismay these hordes
of Summer visitors who overcrowd their pavements,
overfill their carparks and take up
their right of way.
They annoyed think that locals should have precedence
in crowded shops and banks;
they never think that these visitors deserve our thanks;
the more these visitors come, stop and shop,
the more they prop up one of Scotland's
most vital industries – one of the last that survives.
These visitors play an important part in keeping
this Perthshire town alive, we should rejoice that so many
come to Pitlochry, that many, returning year after year,
make it their Mecca, an unspoiled place they treasure
for their sedate holiday pleasure.

Our hoteliers, shopkeepers and restaurateurs,
also our festive theatre's bright thespians
surely all deserve our utmost praise as they fight
the desperate battle against their sun-blessed foreign rivals,
and, unwearied, help carry part of the burden
of our small country's economic survival.

As more and more of these welcome visitors come
and repeatedly return may our restaurants, hotels and shop,
our theatre, our many hospitable welcoming B&B's,
and all in this vital leisure industry
win another bumper Summer crop and rejoice
in one more vital harvest once more won.

Evolutions Web

This lovely small lochan is serene home of Mallard,
Moorhen and Coot;
here many Mallards, with wide-webbed orange red foot,
with effortless movements that are efficiently neat,
truly belong, are comfortably at home
in their watery element where drakes heads of dark bottle-green
sudden turn and instant become
a new beauty of an iridescent glowing purple sheen.

Also displaying controlled watery ease are these graceful Coots
that are much less sure or neat on land as they
cautiously place each jerky foot's
semi-webbed awkward grey toes that are so
squashily ungainly as they flop then flatten.
Perhaps these Coots gradual spreading partial webbing
is slowly surely following Mallards long evolved
sure-footed route.

Following much slower in Nature's evolutionary challenge
is the hesitant Moorhen which on uncertain water
forever awkward nods its doubtful head,
then on land has to meet evolutions demanding race
with anxious and labourious uncertain pace
and with thin webless feet that are inefficient
in water and seem ungainly on land.
It seems you, poor Moorhen, are unsure what to aim for –
water or land, which should be your correct domain?

Uncertain fowl, undecided Moorhen, in future years
will you become a true aquatic, or true terrestrial bird?
Land or Water? Will you be sure you have correctly
fulfilled your life's mission...
even then made the correct evolutionary decision?

Standing Stones

Four thousand, or more, years have passed since
Pagan Picts painstaking placed these large grey stones on end.
Did they heated discuss where to set them?
Did they argue over how many to place in this new stone circle?
Were these Standing Stones profound religious symbols?
Did solemn Picts here wonderingly ponder life's deep mystery?
Safe enclosed within these stones did they hesitant
discuss their tribal loves,
then with much more heated passion retell
their ancient tribal hates?
After the passing of so many years everything these Picts
so passionately discussed and so fiercely argued
now seen so terribly petty;
all these once vividly alive Pagan religious themes
are now seen as merely foolish illusory dreams.

After another four thousand years have passed
will our present proud civilizations
so many conflicting religions fare any better?
Will they too go into terminal decline,
be unable to withstand the relentless test of time?

Will all our all too many Churches, Chapels and Synagogues,
all our far too many Temples and Mosques –
each proclaiming their own God the only True God –
all too be lost, become almost completely forgot,
become nothing but so many empty spaces
encircled by a few tenacious old grey stones?

Skylark

Standing enthralled I watch that Skylark rise ever higher
until that pilgrim speck of vertical flight
magic melts into sky's pure azure light
but yet pours down that unmatched song
that overwhelms all who hear with receptive ear.
It seems absurd that one small inconspicious dowdy bird
can so marvellously transform itself into this wonder
of nothing but pure cascading bliss.

Surely only the spiritually dead, those bereft of beauty
would try to assure us that this Skylark's song
is merely part of that bird's claiming of territory,
nothing more than instincts demanding duty.
How can they hear such marvellous notes flood fourth
and yet deny that lark something like a soul,
some hidden thing that's passionately alive with beauty?

Suddenly – cut as with a knife – my lark
shuts off its divine praise of Life;
goes into free fall, drops like guided stone
until braking wings fling it to his mate
snug on eggs in her heathery home.

Then again my rising lark's song bursts forth
and I again stand enthralled and must once more wonder
how you can fashion such urgent passion...
Such joy, such hope...
Such happy urgings and tremulous surgings
that come high-transcending, never ending
tumbling and jumbling from your tiny throat.

Surely there's little assistance required from those quivering wings,
that joy you sing, that power outpouring
is alone enough to keep you soaring!
Almost motionless poised you are no longer bird
of flesh and blood...
Are pure tempestuous flood of divine voice!

My soul now soars and, fantastically madly unbound
by my lark's rapturous sounds,
goes ever higher soaring and, free of all terrestrial cares,
blissful shares that pure, translucent
transcendental blue with you.

Violated Ben Vrackie

Poor violated Ben Vrackie, it seems an awful shame
that you no longer live up to your correctly given name.
Ben Vrackie in Gaelic means 'The Speckled Hill',
but practically all the sparkling white quartz rocks
that once were most plentifully, conspicuously
and attractively scattered across your steep slopes
and earned you that name are long since gone...
Are now to be found in many an old Pitlochry rockery
set in neat Victorian gardens mature lawn.

Your slopes have been disrespectly plundered
by irreverent Victorian rock–garden hunters...
ruthless violators who disliked these bright speckled rocks
wide scattered natural disorder.
They vigorously set out and tamed them;
set them in strict regimented, neat, staid,
properly conforming Victorian order.

Red Squirrel

No matter how often previously seen surely it's impossible
not to gasp with uplifting delight
at each fresh sight of active scampering, fast chattering
and tree-top leaping Red Squirrel?

Oh of course it's all too easy to be led astray
by all that 'bright eyed and bushy tailed' effortless,
almost Disneyish, charm,
but isn't there perhaps less harm
in this than being all too cooly scientific
in our reaction?

Shouldn't 'Beauty's Truth' be our constant aim?
Surely it would be a terrible shame
if we ever failed to emotionally thrill
at sight of an active scampering Red Squirrel!

Dawn Fawns

Gently easing myself into the shadowy cathedral
of these tall pine trees I stand obscure in their dappled shade
while dawn's slanting sunshine
spotlights a sleepy bracken glade.

I wide-eyed gaze as a grazing roe deer flows on stage.
That alert maternal doe's feeding progress is contentedly slow,
is happily hampered by her tiny twin fawns.

How gloriously all three of these russet coats glossily gleam
in dawn's wondrous shimmering forest beams,
how all their bright snowflake spots
glow a mini-blizzard of delight
in virgin mornings pure translucent light.

This scene of perfect living beauty is all the more perfect
for lasting only a very short time...
It glowed for little more than one minute,
one sublime, breathless vivid minute
then the doe gently guides her tiny twin fawns
and all instant vanish into high brackens
concealing verdant green fronds.

Exceptional Visibility
(On Ben Vrackie, Saturday, 21st August, 1999)

At a steady, sweaty, plodding pace
we've laboured up Ben Vrackie's obdurate South face
and now we thankful stand on graceful summit.
Standing in thin, clear, azure sunshine we're amazed
and elated by the endless vastness of surrounding space.
There's no mist, no rain, no heat haze to obscure this day's
truly exceptional visibility and so, awed to silence,
we continue standing, continue gazing at this
'our own, our native land' while limitless space
reveals infinite beauty, reveals what almost seems
half of this ancient land.

Supreme Ben Nevis, brave glowing in the distant West,
proud flaunts what seems a remnant of its almost eternal snows
or might be a clinging wisp of white mist.
By Loch Tummel Schiehallion raises its elegant pyramid,
beyond dark Rannoch's peat stained moors
haunting daunting Glencoe thrusts up its defiant fists.
Further South, Ben Lawers rises bright and clear,
then, beyond many bluish ridges and hidden glens,
Ben Lomond defiant peers through the crystal atmosphere.

Moving East towards Edinburgh our eyes seek, then greet
the modest steep of Arthur's Seat;
then we see the Sidlaw Hills rise and hide
the couthy city of Dundee.
Further North the crouching Cairngorms reveal those
fine, undulating high plateaus
that wear a delicate hue of mountain-hare blue.

Our eyes now seek no further peaks,
silent, euphoric, we dare not speak
for fear of shattering this fragile almost mystic state.
Engulfed in the prodigious might of this fabulous light
we let Nature's purest art uplift our responsive hearts,
let Eternal Nature fulfill its highest role
of enriching our all too ephemeral human souls.

Ben Vrackie

The Golf Course Ghost
(A Story)

While concentrating on where I was going in the confusing grey dimness of this shrouding Autumnal mist I occasionally paused, stared into the mist and tried to assure myself that it did seem to be slightly clearing. Perhaps this was more wishful thinking than true experienced observation, for in a minute or two that mist perversely got even thicker.

Should I push on and climb Craigower Hill or should I turn back and keep on lower ground? While pondering these questions, I continued on the grassy track that was the right-of-way across Pitlochry golf-course. Even this well known route seemed at times vaguely unfamiliar as dense grey mist mysteriously moved things out of their usual place.

Perhaps foolishly, I decided to push on . I felt reasonably confident that this morning's mist would soon clear away. Concentrating on exactly where I was going, it was reassuring to have the golf course's boundary fence to my right; and I knew there was a deep ditch to the left which I'd been keeping wary of.

Suddenly I saw a dim uncertain thing silently loom up from the mist-shrouded ground.

Startled, frightened, I staggered back. A voice – thankfully a normal human voice – said, 'Hello there'. Somewhat reassured, I cautiously moved forward. That voice repeated, 'Hello there,' then added, 'Oh, is that you, Robert?'

I gasped, 'Aye, it is,' then with a relieved laugh said, 'You gave me a hell of a fright, Bill. I thought you were a ghost rising up out of a grave there!' Bill's laughter joined mine, 'No, I'm nae ghost. And this is nae grave. It's this damned deep ditch I'm clearing out.' He scrambled out of the ditch and stood beside me.

Bill was a greenkeeper on this golf-course. We often met and stopped and talked as I climbed this path on my frequent visits to my favourite local wee hill, Craigower.

Grinning, Bill now said, I'm sorry I frightened you. Did I really look very vague, ghostly and wraith like?'

I again laughed, 'Aye, you did then. You certainly don't now!' Nor did he as the solid bulk of his over six feet tall body overshadowed me.

'Anyway,' Bill said, 'this is not where you'd expect to see a ghost on this golf-course. It's at the Picts Fort near the fourth hole that you're more likely to see one.'

'Oh, why? Is that ancient fort haunted? Have you seen a ghost there, Bill?'

'No I haven't. But my wife, Bella, has!'

I smiled sceptically and quizzically.

'Aye, she has. I believe her. Aye, and our tough wee fox-terrier, Tam, certainly saw that ghost tae!'

I persuaded him to tell me about that ghostly sighting.

'It happened late in a bright sunny June evening last year after all the golfers were finished. Bella took wee Tam a stroll over the deserted golf-course. She was just out to enjoy the lovely Summer evening. She had no thoughts of anything ghostly.'

Bill paused then asked me, 'You've been at the site o' that Pictish Fort, haven't you?'

'Oh aye I have. I've had a good look at it, but I never saw any ghosts there.'

'No, perhaps not. Anyway, to continue my story. Bella was sitting on one of the large stones marking the site of that ancient Fort with wee Tam lying relaxed at her feet. Both were quietly contentedly enjoying their rest in this lovely place with its fine views down Strathtummel.

'Then with startling suddenness a strange silent figure appeared as if up from the ground only a few yards below where Bella was sitting. That figure was a man, but a strange wild looking man. He had a long, wildly bushy beard and his head's straggling dark hair seemed to intermingle with that beard in unruly confusion. His voluminous cloak or plaid and baggy trousers seemed all made of thick coarse wool of a fawnish brown colour.

'For a few moments he silently stood and stared at Bella. These moments seemed a petrified eternity to her. Then she turned and ran. She did not stop running until she was safe at home with me.'

Bill's story was finished, he waited to hear what I would say.

'This strange man, this "ghost," did or said nothing more?'

Bill laughed, 'No, he didn't. Bella did not stay to try and make polite conversation with him.'

'And he was definitely dressed like an ancient Pict?'

'Aye, he was exactly like pictures of them Bella and me have seen in books.'

'And he rose up out of the ground in front of Bella?'

'Aye, he did.'

I smiled sceptically, 'Just like you ghostly rose up out of that "grave" just now, eh? Oh, Bill, don't you think that "ghost" was most probably some wild tramp or backpackers who'd been lying on the grass in a hollow out of sight of Bella who suddenly frightendly got to his feet?'

Bill reluctantly nodded his head, 'Aye, I suppose that's possible. But what about his ancient Pictish clothes?'

I laughed, 'Oh, Bill, when you see how strangely many of those wandering, long-bearded filthy tramps are dressed, and some wild, rough-sleeping backpackers are little better, then surely they wouldn't look much different from some ancient Picts.'

Bill grinned and agreed, 'Sure that's true. Aye, and some o' thae young Hippies fair dress gae queer too!' He thoughtfully paused then quietly asked, 'But how do explain wee Tam's strange reaction if that was nae ghost he and Bella saw?'

I had forgotten about the terrier, Tam. I asked, 'Well, and how did he react?'

'You know what wee Tam's like don't you? He's a real tough and fearless fox-terrier, yet he's quite friendly with every one. Had that not been a Pictish ghost but had been merely a tramp or wild backpacker, Tam would have fiercely barked and challenged them, then, if they were friendly, would have made friends of them. But he did nothing like that.'

'Well, go on What *did* he do?'

Bill smiled and resumed, 'While Bella and the Pictish Ghost were silently staring at one another Tam did not bark or challenge, instead he turned tail and fled for home as fast as his legs could take him.

'I heard him frantically clawing at our house door and when I let him in he completely ignored me and fled straight to his basket with his tail down between his legs. He curled up there violently shivering. When, amazed and worried, I went to questioningly pet him he looked up at me with eyes that seemed to stare with pleading puzzlement and real fear.

'On all their many walks together, Tam had never left Bella and come back home on his own. As I started preparing to go in search of her, Bella arrived. Panting, flustered, exhausted, she collapsed onto the sofa and gasped out her extraordinary story.'

Bill stood silently staring at me for a few moments then smiled and asked,

'Now you who don't believe in ghosts, how do you explain poor wee Tam's obviously terrified behaviour?'

I had no answer.

A Strange Silence

A strange silence pervades this empty air through which
yesterday's Autumn Swallows had so restless soared,
endless soared and scythed their mystic sky
with keen, razor sharp wings.
Now the delicious charm of their exhilarating flight,
all their sweet showers of twittering song
are seen and heard no more.
No Swallows now thrill past gable's jutting eaves,
none fast skim mere inches above harvest's grasses;
obeying urgent natural urgings, they're all sudden gone.

Bare are those high, tight-stretched wires
where often rested those flocks of Summer Swallows
that festooned each wire with blue/black musical notations
that composed an insubstantial score's
profoundly endearing creation.
I wish them well on that long, hazardous, Southern flight
that for some will be a final journey into Death's dark night.

Strange this sudden silence - strange, not sad
for hushed space yet strangely vibrates
with those departed Swallows swooping grace.
They seem to have left behind a vivid remembrance
of those drowsy Summer days when they dramatically
acrobatically skimmed calm waters sparkling surface,
and they have also left their promise
that in the not too distant future
they will once more start their return Northern flight,
will bright wing their certainty of bringing
next year's eager Spring.

Autumn Tartans

Bright draped in Autumns multi-hued plaid
Perthshire proud displays its tartan glories.
Every Rowan's heavy load of brilliant berries
join with arterial leaves to flaunt
their flamboyant clan's Royal Stewart reds;
these vivid colours glow all the brighter when seen
beside massed armies of marching Firs
that swaggering wear their regimented Black Watch greens.
And those many drifts of sturdy Larch and slender Birch
do their utmost to attract by boldly wearing
the glaring yellows of the MacLeod of Lewis.

High thin clouds fling down those fleeting shadows
that race and chase across the radiant glowing glory
of this Autumnal landscape and seem to spread out
their plaid of ever changing light and shade,
a plaid that suggests the rather confusing pattern
of the Chattan Clans rather gaudy tartan.

As ever more of Perthshire's heather moors
are smothering smoored under ever more
aggressively invasive Bracken, that iniquitous weed
celebrates its victory by wrapping those depleted moors
in glaring tartaned pleats of boastful bronze and gold
that we guess are copied from the glaring Dress Macmillan tartan.

Perthshire lochs are resigned to being unable to compete
with surrounding lands tartaned plaids and pleats,
yet do not want to be quite left out of all this bright
Autumnal Extravaganza, so they modestly wear
the subdued, gently faded blue tartan of the Elliot Clan
and thus neatly complete this unique
Autumnal Gathering of The Clans.

Northern Lights

Call them what you like: the Northern Lights,
the Aurora Borealis, the Heavenly Dancers,
whichever name you use their fantastic beauty remains the same.
See them glare iridescent bright
in the vastness of the Northern Night;
see their vivid flaring rainbowed beams
advance, retreat, then again meet.
This glorious show is brought about
by immense burst of Solar Radiation...
radiation which emits much Light but no Heat.

How different from poor auld Scotland's
bright new Northern Lights so comfortably ensconced –
at astronomical cost –
in Edinburgh's brand-new Parliament.
With what passion, with what righteous might
they rant and have their say,
but I fear that at the end of each day
it's always the same...
They've emitted much Heat but no Light!

Fantastic Natural Artist

Autumn – that fantastic natural artist – careless scatters
its fabulous bohemian madness;
it drips rowans berried blood, transfuses anaemic leaves
to arterial reds; slants quixotic sun's
dust–dancing lances at exotic targets;
turns leafy oak's iron strength to decaying rust.
Makes chanterelles blare their triumphant yellow trumpets,
discharges terrific overnight explosions of all sorts
of fungi with wonderful exultant abandon
then – perversely changing its mind – melts that attractive
fungi into the repulsive slime of its sad, slow, ugly decline.

This fantastic natural artist now kaleidoscopes
a bright effusion of stained–glass over lochs,
sets Mallards attractive floating not on still waters,
but on narcissistic mirrored hills.
As that land and this water confusing fuse and blend
it's impossible to tell where hill begins, where loch ends.
As solid reality melts into surrealistic light
our neat dividing line between pike and pine
is confuted by this natural artist's magical palette.
All this fantastic magic awakes a confusing Blake
of mysticism; our thrilled spirits soar with aesthetic delight;
our souls know grand exotic flights.
But we are also vaguely aware of some primordially deep
sensual senses which – hinting at forbidden Pagan pleasures –
threaten to transform logic's neatly arranged order
into dreadfully attractive Dinosaurish disorder.

Contrasts

What an amazing contrast those two lairs are.
The fox's den is an untidy stinking slum,
is fouled with cubs and adults plentiful droppings,
is littered with discarded wings of grouse, of gulls,
and of an unfortunate crofter's slaughtered hens.
Surrounding heather is festooned with wind-scattered feathers,
lambs pathetically skinny wooly legs are snarling cubs playthings.
Larger, thicker, skeleton bare bones are the glaring
honed, well chewed remains of an old braxy ewe.

The badgers sett shows no sign of such careless neglect,
it is always neat and tidy except when being spring-cleaned
when precious heaps of dry bedding - harvested grasses
and golden bracken - are set out to air.
Just how fastidiously clean those badgers are is seen
by following the well used track which leads through
high verdant bracken to their discreetly concealed
neatly hygienic latrine.

In the past I admired the fastidious badgers immaculate sett,
but now, getting old, living quietly contentedly on my own,
I like their over-tidy homes much less.
I am increasingly ever more reluctant to waste what little time
- that even more precious time - that is left to me
on doing ever more dreary boring housework.
Glancing around my dustily untidy neglected room I grin,
it's obvious that I now sympathize less and less
with the house-proud badger,
but more and more take after
the careless uncaring, contentedly untidy fox!

My Old Assynt Map

Clearing out an untidy cupboard I sudden re-discovered
my long lost, half-forgot grand old Assynt map.
I smile and wholehearted approve as I see that pre-war
Ordnance Survey Map neatly use the good old scale
of one inch to one mile,
and, completely unaware of these Brussels decreed
modern metres, blithely measures ancient Suilven's
imposing and inspiring steep
in that grand tale of good old Imperial Feet.

As I gently unfold that wind-tattered, rain-stained,
sleet-battered fragile old map, it in turn unfolds
countless memories in my maybe getting slightly fragile
age-assaulted brain.
Spread out on the floor it impetuous flings open many doors
then because a magic carpet that instant wings me back
to Assynt, that vivid brings alive so many memories
of long-past years, of mirth happy or death sad tears,
of oh so many long-dead Assynt friends.

This old Assynt map is not only time and weather stained
and tattered, but has been violent attacked
by a measle rash of red dots.
These dots, and many other more mysterious,
almost Masonically obscure marks, signs and symbols
all tell tales that even I now have some trouble
to correctly decipher.

Then as I sit, deep ponder, and strict instruct my thoughts
not to wander, many correct clear memories
come eager rushing to my aid and with jigsaw
neat precision fit things together...
times, places and people; birds, animal and fish;
the terrible strains of Winter's horizontal rains;
the glorious joys of nightless June's ceaseless sunshine.

Each of these many small red dots pinpoints a gamekeeper's
well-known fox den; these larger, far fewer, dots
mark fastidious badgers tidy setts;
yet fewer secret signs are otters secretive holts,
one special marked lochan is where, more than once,
we've seen playful otters fling themselves in and
streamline through clear water like a silent salvo
of silvery torpedoes.
And that red dot and cross in the Wolf Glen
marks what became a fox den after the last
Assynt wolf was shot; then later it was site
of almost wolfish wild Assynt men's
illicit whisky still and fabulous drinking den.

As, befitted their regal status, golden eagles craggy eyries
well deserved these special marks on my map,
but I sudden wonder might these splendid birds
now be enraged at being upstaged
by these even more splendid sea-eagles
that have now re-colonized these map-marked
coastal eyries their ancestors had once used?

Now my eyes and thoughts grasshopper leapt
from piratical sea to the bright remembered treasures
of Assynt's fresh-water lochs that are accurately
widespread scattered over my old map in such abundance
as to show what seems as much trout-rich water
as wildly rugged land.
And what a kaleidoscopic riot of marks and colours
grace many special lochs and lochans
while one especially favourite place is honoured
with a very special symbol that is consecrated
not only to Eileen's and my own deep love of fishing
but also to the joyous glory of our deep true love's new-wed bliss.

As I start to fold away my Old Assynt Map
I sadly happily nostalgically sigh as I think
of how many smiling Assynt miles that tattered old map
and a much younger, much fitter me have covered together
and so I put it away, not in back of untidy cupboard,
but in a place of honour in my special bookcase
cosily cheek by jowl with my Pitlochry Map.
This comparatively new, barely marked, almost virgin pure
Pitlochry Map can no way compare with my Old Assynt Map,
but I'm truly thankful to it for opening up to me
the far more sheltered calm, the gentle tree-rich verdant
lushness of this beautiful Perthshire districts sedate charms
where, hopefully, I will quietly and contentedly calmly
live out my final years.

Here perhaps over these remaining years Perthshire
will put its mark on me, but surely not quite so
passionately deeply as Assynt put its uniquely distinctive
marks on me, while I in turn left my marks not directly
on Assynt, but, by proxy, on my old Assynt Map.

Two Dukes
(A Story)

Taking my usual walk by Loch Faskally, I once again met Fergus. We stopped and talked. I always enjoyed these talks with Fergus. He was one of the few true natives of Pitlochry, while I, like so many others, had only moved here after my retirement. I gently steered the conversation towards the 'good old days'. I greatly enjoyed hearing Fergus's reminiscent stories of his working and leisure years in Pitlochry and surrounding district.

Today he told me some of his experiences when working on the Duke of Atholl's huge estate at Blair Castle many years ago.

Then I listened with real amusement but with amazement as Fergus told a story he had heard there about a fierce encounter between a previous Duke and a local poacher.

Stopped by the Duke and accused of salmon poaching on his River Tilt the fiery-tempered poacher had almost come to blows with His Grace.

The Duke reported him to the local policeman and had him charged with poaching and assault. That poor poacher spent some days in Perth jail.

Once Fergus finished his story I laughed then exclaimed, 'Oh surely such encounters between a Duke and a salmon poacher must be quite common in the Highlands.'

'Oh why,' Fergus asked, 'have you heard this story of a Duke of Atholl before?'

'No, not the Duke of Atholl, but I do know a similiar story about a past Duke of Sutherland. I heard it when I was living in Assynt.'

Fergus wanted to hear that story. I told him it: It happened a few years before the First World War. Donald Sutherland was a crofter living near Lochinver village. The salmon filled River Inver flowed irresistibly close to his croft. Donald delighted in outwitting the gamekeepers guarding the river. Time after time, using the utmost ingenuity, he snatched a salmon almost under their noses and got clean away with it.

The head gamekeeper, Ewan Grant, hated Donald and vowed to catch him red-handed one day and have him jailed.

The Duke of Sutherland was having a sporting holiday on his Assynt

Estate. Late one afternoon as he was walking away from his River Inver with his 'tail' of retainers behind him, Grant carrying His Grace's fishing rod and two younger gamekeepers loaded with the fine salmon the Duke had caught, they almost bumped into Donald Sutherland as he came round a sharp bend on the path beside the river. Both parties stopped and stood staring at one another. Donald stood none too steadily, his breath reeked of whisky, obviously he had been happily partaking of a few drams.

'Where are you going? What are you up to?' the Duke commandingly demanded to know.

Anger flared in normally placid Donald, he was not accustomed to being spoken to like that. 'Och, I'm taking a walk up by the river as I've every right to do.'

'Oh, going poaching, are you? Going poaching on my river?'

'Your river?. Your salmon? Your land and your sun and sky, I suppose? You own everything, don't you?'

His Grace flushed with anger. He too was not accustomed to being spoken to like this. With bad grace he ignored this outburst and turned to his head gamekeeper, 'Search him, Grant. No doubt he has a gaff or a net hidden somewhere about his person.'

'Yes, your Grace,' Grant obsequiously replied. He carefully laid down his master's fishing rod then eagerly stepped up to Donald.

Donald innocently held out his arms, 'Go on, search me. Search me as much as you like.'

Almost trembling with disappointment, Grant reported, 'He's got nae poaching gear on him, your Grace.'

'Are you sure?... Oh doubtless he has it hidden somewhere nearby.' The Duke snarled, 'Haven't you got it hidden, you... you, what's your name?'

'My name is *Mr.* Sutherland, your Grace,' Donald over-polite announced.

'Well, Sutherland, isn't your poaching gear hidden nearby?'

Swaying slightly, Donald tried not entirely successfully to look complete innocent, 'No it isn't. I don't ken what you're talking aboot.'

As the annoyed Duke started to walk past Donald he loudly commanded, 'Well, Sutherland, don't let me see you here again at my salmon river.'

Stepping in front of him, Donald stopped his Grace, 'Your river, your land? By rights it's as much my land and river as yours. Your accursed family stole it from us, your ain clansmen, and gave it tae your bloody sheep.'

The Duke tried to walk on but again Donald stopped him and passionately asked. 'Aye, and what about all the clansmen who for centuries fought and died for their clan chief, shouldn't their descendants have received more consideration from your family?'

The angered Duke vehemently snarled, 'Do you think the Chiefs didn't fight too? My family fought for centuries to gain and hold this Sutherland land.'

'Oh, did they now?' Donald excitably cried, 'Well, I tell ye what I'll dae – I'll fight ye for it here and now. Come on!... Come on!'

The Duke and his gamekeepers looked on in amazement as Donald threw off his tweed jacket, raised his clenched fists and advanced on his Grace in a boxing posture loudly shouting, 'Come on!.. Come on! Raise yer fists an' fight like a man!'

With his fists jabbing the air Donald circled around the Duke with what imagined was an experienced boxer's fancy agile footwork but was in reality more a staggering uncertain soft-shoe shuffle. He repeatedly challenge, 'Come on!... Come! Fight like a man!'

Each time he tried to get away the Duke found Donald blocking the path.

'Oh, damn it,'his Grace cried in exasperation, 'I've had enough of this ridiculous nonsense!' He turned to his gamekeepers, 'Grant, Fraser, MacLaren, apprehend this drunken oaf and frog march him to Lochinver police station. I'll go ahead and alert the local policeman. I'll have this obnoxious wastrel charged with being drunk and disorderly and threatening physical assault.'

'Yes, your Grace,' Grant keenly replied, delighted at the prospect of Donald Sutherland being jailed at last.

As the gamekeepers grabbed Donald the Duke strode disdainfully away and Donald shouted after his retreating figure, '*Your Grace?... Your Grace?...* You're nothing but a *bloody disgrace,* your Grace!' Delighted with this sudden inspired expression, he repeatedly called out, 'Aye, you're nothing but a bloody disgrace!'

'Och, be quiet you damned fool,' ordered head-gamekeeper Grant as the two younger gamekeepers firmly held Donald by his arms.

'Och, bugger you, Grant, you arse-kissing toady. I'll no' fight wi' you; I want tae fight the organ-grinder, no' his bloody monkey!'

This insult struck home especially keenly as Grant was all too well aware of the nickname his enemies had given him – 'The Hairy Ape'. He certainly was very hirsute with his large beard, his bushy eyebrows, hairs growing from ears and nostrils and thickly matting the backs of his hands. With mischievous glee Donald added to his insult, 'Och, I suppose you're mair a bloody hairy ape than a damned monkey. I'll grant ye that, Grant!'

Grant swore at him then turned furiously on the two younger gamekeepers who could not prevent themselves from grinning. 'Whit the hell are you twa laughing at? You'll hae something tae laugh aboot if I get ye sacked, won't ye?'

They instantly fell solemnly serious. This was no light threat. The possibility of losing their jobs was truly no laughing matter for these young men. They had their wives and bairns to think of. If they lost their job, they also lost their gamekeepers 'tied' estate house, and if the Duke was displeased with them they might well be blacklisted and find themselves unable to get a job on any other estate.

Donald Sutherland was duly charged, tried and sentenced. He spent fourteen days in Dornoch jail.

When he was released from jail Donald found he had become a living legend. The story of him having challenged the Duke of Sutherland to fight for his land had swept across the entire country. By the time this tale reached Caithness, Ross-shire and Inverness rumour's wild exaggerations had done their inevitable work – Donald had knocked his Grace unconscious; it had required a posse of policemen and gamekeepers to overcome and arrest him. Donald received a hero's welcome when he returned to Lochinver. Innumerable drams were forced on him and countless admiring toasts drunk to him, to 'Donald Disgrace', as he had already been firmly nicknamed. He proudly retained that name until his death at a ripe old age.

★ ★ ★

Fergus laughed as I finished my story, 'That's quite a coincidence, isn't it? Your story of 'Donald Disgrace' challenging the Duke of Sutherland is practically the same as my story of the Duke of Atholl being challenged by a local poacher. But as far as I know, that Atholl poacher acquired no nickname for his daring exploit.'

I now laughed, 'Aye, it seems a real coincidence right enough. Or perhaps stories of poachers challenging Dukes have become legendary. Perhaps they have been told and endlessly re-told about every landowning Scottish Duke.

Scarlet Seduction

How terribly flamboyantly these Rowan trees
display their fiery Autumn finery;
how forwardly and with such passionate vulgarity
they unashamedly smear on their vivid lipstick reds
then how unwholesomely erotically they whore-rouge
their sensual, falsely blushing leaves.

Little wonder that those wildly excited Northern flocks
of Norse-fled Fieldfares and Redwings
can not resist those gaudy trees
but become easy victims of all this scarlet seduction.
With what lusty Viking vigour they plunder
and red-bloodied satiate themselves
on all this luscious seductive fare
then, completely uncaring, leave their
victims stripped bare.

It seems rather sad that these Rowan trees
should be so ruthlessly stripped naked,
their berry-less and leaf-less branches
left stark silhouettes shivery exposed
to Winters cruel advances.

Oh but those violently violated raped and gobbled
Rowan berries have the last laugh
as, white coated with Fieldfare manure,
their tough seeds are widespread scattered
and will in time become healthy thriving Rowan saplings.

'I to The Hills....'

Dismal December's early descending dusk bleak smothers
the small town of Pitlochry where, along almost deserted streets,
a few winter-weary pedestrians hurry, hunch and scurry
against an icy wind that threatens to bring more snow
or fling even more cruel flurries of slithery sleet
and make even more slick that oilskin glitter
these soaking pavements wear and further fill these
mucky runnels and bloated gutters that so slushily gurgle
their deep-throated sadistic chuckles.

Almost none of those hurrying few who scurry past those old,
cold Victorian buildings think to lift their gaze
from this place of winter dreary dismal streets
to where Ben Vrackie clear rises above this town's
dusk drowned frowning misery and nobly glows
with sunsets delightful pulsing light.

Those very few who do stop, who stand and stare
with uplifting eyes are inspired by Ben Vrackie's
sudden ephemeral splendour as that hill's thick snows
bright flare and momentarily vivid glow
as this sunset puts on its splendidly brilliant show.
To those spellbound watching few this hill's
sudden, brief, magical mystical glowing
gives rise to thoughts and feelings far beyond anything
downcast dull eyes and dull downcast minds can ever know.

Christmas Card List

That row of names before me is not just
my Christmas Card List
but is a toll of passing years,
of ever victorious Death,
of dear old friends departed,
of sad shed tears.
Most years I score off a few,
this year another two.
Oh how long – how soon – will it be
before others draw a thick black line through me?

Kingfisher

That sudden seen Kingfisher seems a lightning flash
of iridescent blue that streaks sure and true
over Loch Dunmore and shimmers its very special extra beauty
over this wee Loch's already heady aesthetic treasure.

Then from being a glittery jewel of flamboyant hues
you sudden become a ruthless killer
as, neat perched, you savage batter that vice-gripped minnow
as it violent wriggles its final desperate appeals
of useless, soundless squeals.

Lily Pond, the Cuile, Pitlochry

Wise Buzzards

As I watch four Buzzards effortless lift
on warm columns of air then slowly drift
in lazy circles west of Ben Vrackie
I think these flapless gliding birds
have found the best way to live
as they give this fine display of careless ease
and feline mew their almost purring grace.

As those seeming weightless worry free birds spiral ever higher
through the limitless freedom of their azure sky
I think they must be in deep love with their
free soaring natural life, surely must be unburdened
by any memories of past troubles, be wisely unworried
by any foolish fears of future strife.

I am thankful that I too live unburdened
with any useless ugly lumber of past regrets
and waste no thoughts on pointless worries
over my future years, but with soaring Hedonistic
Pagan pleasures I live with those four Buzzards
in the glorious Present and with eager joy revel in all
that the ever present here and now can give.

Blake And Einstein

('To see a World in a grain of sand,
and Heaven in a wild flower,
Hold Infinity in the palm of your hand,
And Eternity in an hour.')
From 'Auguries of Innocence' by William Blake

That great poetic mystic visionary, William Blake,
searched through his swirling clouds of mystic visions
to intuitively guess at realms as yet missed
by science's greatest Astrophysicists.

Although the meanings of Blake's visionary mystic mysteries
are all too often all too obscurely hidden
at least they point towards realms aglow with Beauty's Purity,
perhaps even towards some Heavenly Divinity.

The immense new Scientific Universe contained
in Albert Einstein's fantastic brain led to realms
as yet un-guessed at, realms that even when explained
by that genius still could not be contained
by lesser scientific brains.

Then when, with reasoning logic's scientific purity,
Einstein propounded his astounding Special Theory of Relativity
to the astounded scientific world
that logic-worshipping community quick drew a direct line
from that pure theory of that fantastic mind
to poor Hiroshima's ghastly atomic Devilry.

Which then the purest wisdom, Blake's or Einstein's?...
Mystic dreams of Heaven or science's evil perverted schemes?

Blanks

Oh how dreadful easily we can be seduced
into a drearily weary life that amounts to little more
that one long, boring, terribly empty blank
in which comatose time and life blankly pass by,
then, when looking back in the final stage
of hideous old age, we find that our life has truly been
little more than one long drawn out pathetic sigh.

Oh, if not for God's sake, then for your own sake
do something real before you die,
something, anything, that's nobler and bolder
than anything you've ever done before.
Fill at least one empty blank; experience something of
the deep pleasure, the bright, life-enhancing gifts
that aesthetic creation gives.

Let words - glorious, urgent, storming and soaring words -
burst inhibitions constraining dam,
let them surge in verse or prose, or both,
let them rage in inky torrents,
urgently creatively flood and fill blank page
after blank page.

Or furiously splash, jab and dab with gloriously thick
oil paints; with nervous energetic brushstrokes
frantically express profound emotions,
thrill to ecstatic happiness as a large blank canvase
wondrously rapturously fills.
Or, delighting in a quieter grace,
let smoother flowing, calmer glowing paint
slow portray a dearly loved face.

Or pore over the neat lines of a blank musical sheet,
attempt to score those brave staves
with a lot of tadpole wriggly squiggly marks.
Rapturously dream a foolish notion that your notations
will harmoniously soar for ever more;
or, forced to admit you are no great composer,
at least learn to play some musical instrument,
go on, thinking yourself wondrously gifted
triumphant blow your own trumpet.

Quick, quick, end blank apathy's miserable trance,
rise, advance, fill some blanks,
give profound thanks for the immense privilege
of being wonderfully alive.
Oh, hurry, hurry, fill at least one empty blank,
fill one you must before being thrust
into your impatient waiting grave's abysmally ugly final blank.

The Price of Fish

Overhearing two young housewives vehemently complain
of the terrible price of this supermarket fish
I sudden wish to tell them the true price of fish;
tell of the times I've scoured wild Assynt shores,
have seen the battered remains of storm-smashed fishing boats,
have discovered and helped recover the sea's reluctant given up
cruelly violated bodies of fishermen;
have seen death's normal ugliness terribly supplemented
by sadistic sea's revolting hideousness,
by disfiguring mutilations inflicted by crawling sea-creatures
and by slithery coiling conger eels.

Yes, surely these two young housewives would complain no more
if they were made to know and feel
something of the real price of fish...
That far too high a price we pay in fishermen's lives!

Dougie's Heron
(In memory of Dougie Petrie)

As Dougie stands there between Pitlochry's two competing banks
where unobservant tourists sit and idly gawk
at the passing throng only he delights to see
that familiar, semi-tame, old grey Heron
that stands semi-hid by rank lushness of these massed weeds
that clothe narrow, shallow, Moulin Burn's modest banks.

Dougie loves to watch that Heron's high-stepping walk,
he admires the engrossed stealth of its beady-eyed stalk,
but even his observant eyes cannot follow the lighting strike
of that bird's keen stabbing beak.
Beset with strange, not unpleasant, conflicting emotions
he keenly watches that doomed small trout's
final futile struggles, he emotionally gulps as that Heron
swallows with urgent gulping need,
with insatiable seeming greed.

Dougie now takes the pleasant short walk to *his* seat
below Pitlochry's two competing charity shops.
Seated at ease, he again delights to see that *his* Heron
is again also making the same short journey.
Ending its familiar flapping flight it steeply falls,
almost seems to stall as it alights near him
in Pitlochry's own small Burn it shares with Moulin.
Then while still trying to neatly fold away
the awkwardness of its ungainly umbrella wings
that Heron is already searching for fresh prey.

As he alertly watches that amazingly skilled natural fisher
Dougie's memories flood him back to far-off youthful times,
to happy days when he was much fitter, was almost as keen
and skilled a fisher as that dirk-beaked bird.
When *his* Heron heaves up and flaps away with labouring wings
and gawky dangling legs, Dougie also heaves himself up
on creaky knees and pain-afflicted hip.

For a short time, slowly, still youthful fish-memory dreamily,
he follows the twist and turns of this now seen,
now unseen modest wee Burn.
Arriving at the restaurant this Moulin Burn flows around
he meets, he greets, is cheerily greeted by this genial places
man and wife team who are his fine kind friends.

Two days later these friends – like so very many others –
shudder under the stark dark sadness
of the unbelievable suddenness
of Dougie's tragic death.

As trembling emotional hands sad scatter Dougie's
wind-bourne ashes over trout-blessed Perthshire waters
and over bright blushing August heathers
all these deep grieving mourners see a Heron – *His Heron?*-
fling up and away; they hear it give a few plaintive
harsh cries as it determinedly soars ever higher
and seems to return to higher Highland heights
and brighter Perthshire Burns.
And these emotional mourners hope that Dougie too
has now soared; has now returned to some higher, wider,
brighter, more trout-filled Perthshire Burn
than Pitlochry's narrow, shallow,
random meandering modest wee Moulin Burn.

Maggie's Mince And Tatties
(For Margaret Drummond)

For many quietly contented retirement years I've been a regular diner
at that restaurant which is Pitlochry's unpretentious best
for outstandingly good home-cooked Scots food.
Many a cold, dreich, winter's day has been brisk transformed
as I'm glowingly warmed by a big bowl of Maggie's
most thick, most braw, steaming hot Scotch Broth.

Often when, after a most generous helping of her mouth-watering
home-made Steak Pie, I protestingly doot
if I'll manage any of her mighty Clootie Dumpling
she will smilingly insist, and, knowing its useless to resist,
I happily acquiesce to her forceful request that I eat up!

For a long time Maggie perseveringly tried to fatten me up;
it's a poor advertisement for her restaurant
that after all those many years of her best braw cooking
I remain so stubbornly thin.
But now she resignedly knows she can never win,
for, despite her best endeavours, all her high heaped plates
of my favourite food – Maggie's most luscious Mince and Tatties –
she now reluctantly accepts the fact
that her best customer will never get fat...
She will never transmute him from being a gaunt Skinny
to being a plump Fatty!

Still Climbing

I still manage to climb some Pitlochry hills;
can still fairly easily manage fine wee Craigower,
but taller, stepper, Ben Vrackie
is now quite a different matter;
its path's new stone steps that stretch
from its wee Loch to near its summit cairn
are quite fine on my upward journey,
but why are they oh so knee-joltingly creakingly
painful on my downward journey?

Yes, its great that I can still climb some lesser
Perthshire hills; can still rejoice in what these hills can give,
and with high hopes I trust this bliss
will continue as long as I live;
but oh, is it me that's getting ever weaker
or are these cheating Perthshire hills
really getting oh so deceitfully ever steeper?

Good Scots Food

Why do so few Scots poets pen their praise
of good Scots Food?
Surely eating good food is one of life's finest treasures;
is the only pleasure that truly last throughout our entire life.
It is with us from when, newly-born, we cosy snuggle,
gurgle and suckle at our almost ecstatic swooning,
love–crooning mother's generous maternal breast.
Then our eager – though maybe meagre – eating becomes
the only pleasure left as we reach our cruel senility,
our sad drooling imbecility.

Only immortal Burns with his 'Great chieftain o' the pudding race!'
gives our good Scots food some much needed praise –
even if only our now disdained, tourist-sought,
too oft' mocked, poor humble Haggis.
The food I would praise is none o' yon tongue-burning,
belly churning, spice-hot curries, nor any o' these
taste-bud teasing and tormenting sweet and sours...
I hae nae truck wi' a' that foreign muck!
The food I love is all Scotland's ain –
the great fish our Brussels oppressed fishermen still gain
from these barely still oor ain stormy Scots seas.
These homely dishes o' crisp grilled Herring;
these uniquely tasty fresh caught Haddies;
that king o' fish, the wild Scots Salmon,
its great taste made oh so much greater
when expertly caught on your own salmon fly-rod.

Then how we're blessed as our good Scots soil
unstinting gives o' its rich best
and these freshest o' braw vegetables fill our winter - conquering
pots o' guid Scotch Broth...
My mouth waters at the very thought!
Then how these high-heaped plates o' mince, tatties and skirling -
- that simple but gloriously good Scots food -
so often, so joyously, sets our delighted taste-buds thrilling.

I must now end these few heartfelt lines
for nagging hunger grumbles that it's past my usual time to dine,
and so I eager hurry to that Pitlochry restaurant
where I'll pleasantly eat, then, replete, restful linger.
I know that there I'll get not merely *good* Scots food,
but that, being not only home-cooked, but 'Mag-cooked,'
it will be truly *Great* Scots Food!

Summoned

(For Margaret and George Drummond)

"But deep this truth impress'd my mind-
Thro' all His works abroad,
The heart benevolent and kind
The most resembles God."
From *'A Winter Night'* by Robert Burns

When Death makes its inevitable call on me,
and, despising my useless pleading resistance,
grim beckons its dread summons
I can only hope that in Heaven –
if that's where I'm to be summoned –
I'll get a welcome as great, as " benevolent and kind"
as I always got at "Drummond's"!

Julio de Santa Ana / Towards a Church of the Poor